THE TEUTONIC MYTHOLOGY
OF
RICHARD WAGNER'S
THE RING OF THE NIBELUNG

Volume I
Nine Dramatic Properties

THE TEUTONIC MYTHOLOGY
OF
RICHARD WAGNER'S
THE RING OF THE NIBELUNG

Volume I
Nine Dramatic Properties

William O. Cord

Studies in the History and Interpretation of Music
Volume 16

The Edwin Mellen Press
Lewiston●Queenston
Lampeter

Library of Congress Cataloging-in-Publication Data

Cord, William O.
   The Teutonic mythology of Richard Wagner's "The Ring of the
Nibelung" / by William O. Cord.
      p. cm. -- (Studies in the history and interpretation of music
; v. 16-)
   Contents: v. 1. Nine dramatic properties.
   ISBN 0-88946-441-3
   1. Wagner, Richard, 1813-1883. Ring des Nibelungen.
   2. Mythology, Germanic. 3. Legends--Germany. I. Title.
   II. Series: Studies in the history and interpretation of music; v.
16, etc.
   ML410.W15C7 1989
   782.1--dc20   89-12612
                                                                CIP
                                                                 MN

This is volume 16 in the continuing series
Studies in History & Interpretation of Music
Volume 16 ISBN 0-88946-441-3
SHIM Series ISBN 0-88946-426-X

A CIP catalog record for this book
is available from the British Library.

The Edwin Mellen Press   The Edwin Mellen Press
       Box 450   Box 67
   Lewiston, New York   Queenston, Ontario
     USA 14092   CANADA, L0S 1L0

          The Edwin Mellen Press, Ltd.
            Lampeter, Dyfed, Wales
          UNITED KINGDOM SA48 7DY

      Printed in the United States of America

To Kim and Chris . . .

May they one day know the feeling
that is ever-present in the *Ring*

TABLE OF CONTENTS

Abbreviations xiii

Note xv

Preface xvii

   I   Wagner, The *Ring*, and Mythology 1

  II   The World Ash Tree 7

 III   The Rainbow Bridge 23

 IV   Donner's Hammer 31

  V   The Tarnhelm 41

 VI   Wotan's Spear 53

 VII   Freia's Golden Apples 63

VIII   Valhalla 71

 IX   The Sword 83

  X   The *Ring* 101

Supplement A   The Ancient Teutonic World
                   and Its Mythology 113

Supplement B   The Sources Of the *Ring* 125

Supplement C   Teutonic Mythology-
                   Some Specifics 133

Index 143

THE TEUTONIC MYTHOLOGY OF RICHARD WAGNER'S

THE RING OF THE NIBELUNG

Volume I: Nine Dramatic Properties

Volume II: The Family of Gods

Volume III: The Natural and Supernatural Worlds

Other books by William O. Cord

José Rubén Romero: *Cuentos y poemas inéditos*
The Futile Life of Pito Perez (Translation)
La vida inútil de Pito Pérez (Editor)
An Introduction to Richard Wagner's Der Ring des Nibelungen. A Handbook
Richard Wagner's The Ring of the Nibelung and Its Teutonic Mythology
Volume II - The Family of Gods

Abbreviations

ME	-	Middle English
MHG	-	Middle High German
Mod. E	-	Modern English
Mod. G	-	Modern German
OE	-	Old English
OLG	-	Old Low German
OHG	-	Old High German
ON	-	Old Norse
OS	-	Old Saxon

Note:

The sources that Wagner used to develop the argument of his drama are also those that served as the basis for the studies of this volume. In the preparation of these essays, it became obvious early on that certain aspects of ancient Teutonic thought, as depicted in these sources, were common to more than one of the individual subject matters under investigation. Whenever that situation arises, that is, whenever one mythological matter is of import in more than one chapter, only the necessary data will be presented in the respective chapters, followed by an asterisk (*). For each item so indicated, a broader, more complete depiction will be found in *Supplement C.*

PREFACE

The dramatic result of Richard Wagner's personal adventures into myth, specifically into that myth of the Teutonic world, was *The Ring of the Nibelung* (*Der Ring des Nibelungen*). Nurtured as he was by the concept that myth was a most appropriate vehicle for dramatic expression, and spurred by his intense belief that myth was the clarion of the true heart and mind of humankind, Wagner created a drama that was, itself, myth. The framework of the *Ring* was myth, its content was mythical, the characters were mythical. Every facet of the poem, figuratively every word, was saturated with the essence of mythical matters that had been the dominant thought of the kindred Germanic peoples so long before.

Before 1876 the world had never experienced such a work as the *Ring*. The response to it was both immediate and overwhelming. There was a tidal wave of reaction that was no less than incredible, a wave that carried in its crest considerations of a dramatic, literary, theatrical, musical, and indeed, of a philosophical and moral nature. In a very real sense, that initial impact has never diminished during the hundred years and more since the *Ring's* premiere performance, and as we enter the second century after its introduction, this drama continues to be a vital and forceful factor in contemporary culture where it continues to exert a magnetic attraction that draws followers of every intellectual and emotional cast.

The persistent and vivid fascination with the *Ring* that is so evident through the years has stirred into action many of those who would know more about the drama. In turn, that action has spawned an almost infinite number of studies which have dealt literally with every conceivable topic that can be associated with the work. One of these many areas of interest and study is, of course, the *Ring* and its mythology. (For a brief history of the ancient Teutonic world, see *Supplement A*.)

The urge to examine the mythology of Wagner's drama has not gone unfulfilled. Over the years, numerous writings on the subject have appeared. Examination of these studies reveals that in the main they have been more generic than particular, more of a general nature in that they have presented what can only be called an overall picture of mythological matters, a kind of superficial approach that excludes a concentrated exploration of a given topic. At such times as writers have attempted to focus on specific factors, their attention usually has been drawn to the more prominent mythological aspects of Wagner's Nibelung poem such as the gods, the Norns, the valkyries, or one or another of the drama's major incidents. Thus it is that despite the interest in Wagner's mythology, and the numerous writings on that subject, there is not currently available a complete and thorough study of the myth contained in Wagner's work, that is, an exhaustive, conclusive examination of *all* the mythological aspects of the *Ring*, their sources, their adaptations, their modifications, their extensions, their blending or fusion, or whatever other treatment the composer gave them. Such a volume (or is it volumes?) that exposes the *Ring* in all its mythical dress remains to be written.

This present volume of essays is a study that takes the reader to a point of mythological understanding that lies somewhere between the extremes offered in the two kinds of works previously mentioned. These essays concentrate on the mythology of certain items that Wagner made integral to his *Ring*. The search into the mythicalness of each of these elements is something more than representative of previous investigations. Every attempt has been made in these studies to present the totality of Teutonic mythological thought that was originally associated with each item, a detailed presentation of function and the relative position of each article within the heathen thought that gave it existence, a comprehension of each item within its original setting.

I call the items of these essays *properties*, a term that has not set well with some of my Wagnerian colleagues, but one which nevertheless seemed appropriate simply because, in theatrical jargon, that is what they really are. And the properties selected for study in this work are indeed prominent ones, articles that cannot be avoided by anyone who approaches Wagner's *Ring*, items that figure dramatically in the argument of the drama.

The primary sources for the mythological data that are presented in these essays are those that served Wagner as he went about the business of creating the *Ring*. Thus it is that *The Poetic Edda*, written in Old Norse, the Icelandic *Volsungasaga*, and the German *Nibelungenlied* are referred to and cited throughout the volume. To a lesser extent, as it was with the composer, the Norse *Thidrekssaga* was utilized when the occasion so warranted. However, yet another work -- one unacknowledged by Wagner -- was brought into the present study. This added work was *The Prose Edda*, a thirteenth-century manuscript by the Icelander Snorri Sturluson. This book has been consulted because it contains certain tales that in the main paraphrase those of *The Poetic Edda*, and others that reveal a singularity of mythological information. (For a discussion of the sources of the *Ring*, see *Supplement B*.)

The presentation or discussion of information contained in these sources can lead to some linguistic confusion. The several languages represented by these works create the possibility that any given proper noun may appear in as many as four distinct language forms. To facilitate an ease of understanding in this matter, the primary spelling of names used in these essays, at least those that are part of the *Ring*, will be the German form. This system will assure conformity with the practice that Wagner himself followed, and such a process will also avoid what would only be utter linguistic confusion if any or all of the many other language versions of these names were to be used. To facilitate even more the matter of comprehension, the only diacritical markings that are used in these studies are the umlauts that are necessary on certain German words.

The mythological data and information that are presented in these essays are but a part of the study. Although such a body of mythical lore and history can be considered to be a valid investigation in and of itself, it serves here also as a basis, perhaps a background, for a greater more comprehensive understanding of Richard Wagner's dramatic treatment of respective mythological elements, which is also presented here in some detail. Together these two mythical perspectives afford unique insight into the composer's beliefs and concepts regarding his culture's ancient thought and its place in his *Ring* drama. At times, when the two mythical tableaux are viewed side by side, it is very possible that some followers of the Wagner drama, those who heretofore have never questioned the mythology of the *Ring*, may experience a certain dramatic discomfort. These studies will show that the mythology that Wagner incorporated into the *Ring* is not always a faithful reproduction of the early thought of the Teutonic people. Readers may also learn that some of the mythology of the *Ring* is the composer's personal arrangement of unrelated matters for his dramatic or thematic convenience. And others may become aware of certain modifications or alterations of Teutonic mythology that Wagner made when he brought these matters into his drama. And there will be those who will be surprised to learn that occasionally what passes for Teutonic mythology in the *Ring* is really not to be found anywhere in Germanic myth, but rather is an element of Wagner's own creation!

In greater perspective, however, when all of the mythological matters of the *Ring* are examined carefully and properly interlaced with the respective Teutonic thought of an early period, two additional considerations will have surfaced. First, there will be the awareness that Wagner's knowledge of the mythological world of his culture was not one of mere objective data; it will become amply evident that this knowledge allowed the composer a profound and sensitive understanding of that Germanic world that once was, and an understanding of the indelible mark that this early culture made on the civilization that followed. Secondly, it will become obvious that Wagner's manner of weaving this early mythical thought into his own argument was nothing less than that of a genius talent, a singular ability that afforded the composer the means to adapt an ancient mythology into the world of his day without abandoning the fundamental concepts as they prevailed in the heathen Germanic scheme of things.

If nothing more, however, perhaps these essays can initiate interest and provoke additional questions about the *Ring*, and thus serve as an invitation for more extended study of the mythology that is to be found throughout the drama. And, who knows, maybe one day that voluminous, exhaustive study of this subject will become a reality!

W.O.C.

Rohnert Park, California

THE TEUTONIC MYTHOLOGY
OF
RICHARD WAGNER'S
THE RING OF THE NIBELUNG

I
WAGNER, THE *RING*, AND MYTHOLOGY

It is quite possible that there are two works that can be called *Der Ring des Nibelungen*. One, of course, is that monumental musico-dramatic work that Richard Wagner had begun in 1848 and finished some twenty-six years later, the same art work that had its premiere in 1876 in the then recently completed Festspielhaus in Bayreuth. The *second Ring* is not known as such because, in truth, it is not a drama, it is not music, and it is not a combination of these arts. Rather, this second *Ring* is the essence of Wagner's words *about* drama, words that define and detail a new kind of drama that was evolving in his creative mind, something that he could call *true* drama.

Wagner's ideas on this *true* drama are to be found in the several lengthy essays that he wrote and published during the years he was working on the *Ring*. During this period he wrote that he had concluded that German culture was intuitively seeking a form of drama that was decidedly different from the standard fare of the day. He insisted that this new drama was a stronger, more intense drama, one that would replace what he believed to be the shallow dramatic stuff that had been placed regularly before German audiences. Wagner was convinced that contemporary drama, at least that drama that formed a part of what routinely was called 'opera,' was directed at the public's superficial understanding, and, he claimed, this drama was fashioned in the mold of the societal manners that were exercised by that public. Thus it was, he reasoned, that any theme of a social nature could be presented only within the context of the artificial societal standards that governed current society. He also believed that any historicity that might be imperative to drama would also be played out in the alien setting of the day, and thus its impact would be lost because the interpretation of that history would be rendered according to these contrived contemporary standards. Wagner claimed that the people were weary of such dramatic mien and manner, that they hungered for *basic truths*, and in the drama of the day such truths were hidden, disguised, distorted, or worse, passed over. The people, he maintained, wanted to *know their self*, and they wanted and expected their drama to give them that portrayal.

The theme of *basic truths* that was so prominent in Wagner's mind caused him to conclude that a more absolute drama was necessary. He envisioned that there would be an examination of *total man* in this new drama. This examination would be of man as he *was*, rather than one that was partial or superficial and then guided by the dictates of a society that had determined how man should be and how he should act in any specific circumstance. Wagner viewed this new drama, this absolute drama, as a sensitive probe of the human experience, a revelation of what he called the "purely human," rather than a drama whose spoken dialogue only displayed humankind within its artificially structured facade. He saw his drama as a presentation of organic emotion rather than a stage piece that addressed itself merely to man's generic exterior feelings. This new drama, as Wagner would have it, would be total drama because it would deal with the quintessence of life, with that which was universal to the human condition.

Wagner had contemplated this distinct type of drama at length and much of his thought was given to the means by which it could be realized. He concluded that the only vehicle that would permit this drama to be brought into existence was *myth*. Myth, he reasoned, was the wisdom of the ages, untouched by temporal societal whims or transitory public fancy. Myth, he contended, represented the universal truth of mankind, a truth that had been filtered, purified, and honed by the aeons of time. Myth, he claimed, was the understanding of all experience.

Wagner spent much time studying the ancient Germanic past, several years in fact, during which he read and analyzed the lays of the gods, the tales of the heroes, and the related studies that eminent scholars had produced. There is no question whatsoever that Wagner was stimulated by the possibilities that these qualities afforded for realization of the type of drama that he promoted. At the same time, he was further excited by a special attribute that he believed he had uncovered in the myth that had flourished within early German culture. As he read the numerous sagas, songs, and poems that are a part of Teutonic mythology, he believed that he had found something of extreme importance to him and significance to the drama that he sought. In addition to the story lines that he came to know, he admitted that he had learned of the heart and mind of German society, the emotional substance of the German character. Now, myth was not only the element by which the dramatic aspirations of the people could become reality, but also the vehicle that could allow for a truly national work, a thoroughly German art, a drama that depicted the vital marrow of the German people and the German nation.

The work that Wagner was evolving in his mind to illustrate his ideas on drama was *The Ring of the Nibelung*. (Curiously, there is some evidence that Wagner's ideas regarding his new art form developed *after* he had thought through the essential matters of his *Ring*, rather than their serving him as a guide for his drama.) Wagner was able to use myth as the foundation for the dramatic argument of his *Ring*. He believed also that with this myth he would be able to explore the *total man* and to present the "purely human" that he thought so necessary to a drama. And, the finished drama would be a national artwork of his native Germany.

The *Ring* was Teutonic mythology. As Wagner told his story of greed, of lust for power, of salvation through love, he turned to the myth that through the years had evolved from the beliefs and thoughts of the ancient ancestors of the German people. Thus, he populated his poem with the figures of the gods and giants and dwarfs and heroes that had occupied the pre-Christian Teutonic mind and which -- each in its own way -- still retained a certain presence in the modern German culture. As he caused these divine and supernatural beings to move about, to act and to react, he made every effort to create for them an ambience that was as mythical as their character, an environment that reflected the eternity that they represented, a world that was untouched by the behavioral veneers of a specious society. Wagner's commitment to myth was total commitment, one that caused him to show the same concern for the lesser matters of that myth that he was to show for the obvious and more significant.

The Ring of the Nibelung was to be, in many ways, a portrait of Wagner's thoroughness in the use of myth. If his drama is replete with mythological figures that are recognized as such immediately, that is, figures, places, incidents, items, and even concepts that are of routine familiarity, it is equally true that the composer wove into his drama a myriad of less prominent aspects of early Teutonic thought. Examples of this latter mythology, which is usually unnoticed by even the most serious students of things Wagnerian, are easily come by; they are to be found literally throughout the *Ring* poem. Every follower of the *Ring* is aware, for example, of certain creatures that are part of the argument, such as a *horse*, a *bear*, a *toad*, and a *dragon*. Few are those persons, however, who can speak to less visual creatures that have their places and their mythological roles in the development of the work, such as the *deer*, the *finch*, and the *wolf*. It is also seldom noted, and usually less understood, that Wagner employed, in strict accord with the mythology, three of the four major points of the compass, *North*, *East*, *West*. He excluded *South*, as did Teutonic mythology, and for good reason. In addition, there are the composer's references to *Hella*, first as the name of the land to which the dead are consigned, and then as the name of the guardian of that land. Wagner also gave a second name to Freia; he called her *Holda*, for reasons of sound and semantics as well as for legendary matters. Readers of the *Ring* cannot help but know of the *World Ash Tree* and its functions. Few, however, are aware that Wagner specified *fir* and *linden* trees at certain points in his poem. Fewer still are those who, if they know of these two trees in the *Ring*, are able to relate the mythological reasons that caused Wagner to place them in his work. These are but a few of the less obvious mythical matters that Wagner incorporated into his drama. They are, nevertheless, representative of the mythical completeness with which he wrote his work, and they attest to the thorough mythical atmosphere that pervades the *Ring*.

Wagner's study of the vast corpus of materials relative to Teutonic mythology had been undertaken with absorbing zeal. In time he came to know the gallery of Germanic divine, supernatural and heroic figures, their relationships, their activities, their functions, and their properties. Wagner also learned of the major as well as the less important incidents within the divine universe and of the beliefs that had persisted about that world. The composer also became familiar with thematic variations of numerous themes that had evolved through the years and he soon became aware of most of the regional interpretations of certain matters of a divine nature. As he read and reread, as he studied and learned, Wagner meditated the situations and committed them to a personal understanding. Then, later, as he actually worked on the *Ring* poem, he would display an amazing talent to recall and then to adapt to his dramatic needs the essence of the mythological world of the early Teutonic peoples. And, Wagner would accomplish these adaptations without exaggeration or fundamental change of the original attitudes.

Wagner premiered his *Ring* in 1876. That premiere, in addition to the presentation of the music-drama itself, was the act of bringing into reality all the words, all the ideas, all the concepts about drama that were contained in the hundreds of pages of his essays. The *Ring* was to be the true drama, the absolute drama that world audiences were demanding. The *Ring* was to depict *basic truths* that he had so often discussed. The *Ring* was to reveal the "purely human" of mankind and to reflect the *total man* that was so necessary in drama. And, as he had written, he attempted to realize these ends with myth and mythology as his dramatic vehicle. It was with that premiere that the two *Rings* of Richard Wagner, the music-drama itself and the essence of his writings about drama, were merged, fused into a single monumental artistic offering. To the extent that Richard Wagner and his *Ring* successfully brought all these matters before the public is a matter of conjecture. It remains fact, however, that with the *Ring* and with Wagner's work in general, world views on opera underwent radical revision and much of the operatic world has since reflected the artistic touch of this genius.

II
THE WORLD ASH TREE

The World Ash Tree, which is a prominent feature in both Eddic literature and Wagner's *Ring*, is -- in effect -- the principal representative of a mythological thought that was strongly influenced, perhaps dominated, by trees. From the earliest days of its history, the ancient Teutonic society was what may be termed a *forest culture*, and, as a result, the oldest form of worship that the society practiced was associated with trees. When one recalls that ancient Teutondom was an expanse of forests and woodlands and also that the people of that society looked upon nature and things natural as being no less than something miraculous, there is little difficulty in understanding why such reverence and veneration developed and persisted, or why such worship held a significant role within the culture.

The concepts that were spawned by this union of Germanic man and the trees that surrounded him are particularized throughout the many myths that have come down to the modern day. The import of trees is nowhere more succinctly apparent than in those myths that offer the Teutonic culture's depiction of the beginning of all things, the creation of the universe. According to ancient Germanic belief, the gods fashioned the natural world from the body of a giant, Ymir. From his eyebrows the deities made Midgard ("Middle Enclosure"), the land in which mankind would have life. The gods then used the giant's flesh to make the soil of Midgard. The deities turned Ymir's blood into oceans, his skull became the heavens and the clouds that floated there were fashioned from his brain. The bones of the giant became the hills, and in great profusion on those hills were the trees that the gods had formed from Ymir's hair. (It seems appropriate to note here that *The Prose Edda* states that the names of the first man and the first woman of the universe were those of trees: *Ask* "Ash" and *Embla* "Elm", respectively. The *Edda* goes on to say that these first mortals were created out of trees.)

The specific reference to *trees* in the heathen Teutonic concept of Creation is indicative of their import in that early culture. This significance becomes even greater when it is noted that *trees* are the only living inanimate objects that are a part of that creation and further, in that beginning, *trees* are closely associated with the supernatural figure *Iord* (Mod. G - *Erde*; Mod. E - *Earth*), who, despite the fact that she did not appear in the hierarchy of divine being was looked upon as the 'mother of all things.'

The veneration of trees by the Germanic peoples became as varied in kind as it was intense. Because of their size, their relative strength, and their general resistance to the furies of nature, trees took on a special role in the primitive rites of worship. The ritual of invocation of the gods, an important practice within the Teutonic beliefs, was regularly carried out within a grove of trees. The signal point of such a service was the sacrifice of an animal. The usual method of sacrifice was hanging. Trees were sturdy enough to accommodate this practice, and there were always available trees of sufficient size and strength to support even the largest of animals. After the sacrifice, the tree afforded a second convenience as the animal's hide was removed and its flesh cut away. (In the early Germanic culture, the only animals that were sacrificed were those whose flesh could be eaten. Wagner incorporated this lesser known aspect of Teutonic practices into the *Ring*. It is in *Götterdämmerung* that Hagen asks that oxen, boar, goat, and sheep be sacrificed to the gods.) Once the sacrificed animal had been stripped, its head could be hung in the tree, or be transferred to another tree, as a highly visible sign of obedience to the demands of the gods for whom the sacrifice had been made.

The tree also served a purpose in the cases of capital punishment. For those condemned to death, the tree was a gallows and regardless of its species it was now called a *wolf-tree*. (The *wolf* was symbolic of outlaws and criminals.) A ritual that usually accompanied this ceremony included an invocation of Wotan, in whose name all hangings were carried out, followed by the smearing of some of the criminal's blood on the trunk as a sign of gratitude for the tree's cooperation. (Two of Wotan's many names were *Hangatyr* "God of the Hanged" and Galgatyr "God of the Gallows".)

The Teutonic attachment to trees was not restricted to matters of death. At times, that attachment could become a reflection of the culture's values. In the early society, war and battle were looked upon almost as a way of life and the warrior was admired and respected above all others of the tribe or village. To recognize an outstanding warrior, one whose sturdiness and strength had resisted the onslaught of determined enemies, that individual could be likened to a tree. One of the greater compliments that the myths have given to a warrior has been to call him the "tree of battle" or "battle tree."

There was yet another quality of trees, in addition to their strength, size, and hardiness, that contributed to their cultural importance. Trees were relatively long-lived, at least when that life span was viewed in relation to that of the people of the day. Such longevity became, in the heathen mind, the equivalent of permanence, a durability that was both unchangeable and immovable. This facet of a tree's existence was then utilized in a practical way as it became the accepted visible means by which boundaries and borders were determined. So profound and so universal did this concept become that vestiges of it are still found in several of the separate Teutonic languages. The Old Norse word for 'forest' was *Marka* (OHG - *Marha*; OE and ME - *Mearc*). In time, as territories and land possessions began to be measured, a forest was easily accepted as a natural dividing line. Thus, the Old Norse word for 'forest' became the word for "boundary," and the word remains, with related meanings in modern German as *Mark*, and in modern English as *mark* and *marker*.

There is, however, no concept, no belief, no practice that exemplifies more vividly the import and significance of this forest culture to the ancient Teutonic peoples than the existence of the runes that were associated with trees. These specific runes were widely known as "tree runes," but a more accurate name was *branch runes* ("limrunar"). The branch runes that are depicted in the Eddic literature refer to the limbs or branches of trees, and more specifically to the magic that these branches were capable of realizing. These runes are a part of the wisdom that Brünnhilde grants to the hero Siegfried after he has awakened her from her sleep, a scene that Wagner adapted as part of the last scene of his *Siegfried*. If much can be offered in the way of description, analysis, and interpretation of this example of the veneration of trees, perhaps the Eddic verses themselves best convey the import they held within the culture. In one of the Eddic poems, Siegfried has ridden up the mountain, crossed through the flames, and entered a tower in which he finds a figure that lies sleeping. He removes the helm from the figure's head, and discovers that the figure is a woman. This person is really Brünnhilde, although in this tale she is called Sigrdrifa, a name applied by the unknown collector of these verses who obviously mistook the epithet *sigrdrifa* ("bringer of victory") as a proper noun. Sigrdrifa awakens, greets the light of day, and then Siegfried learns that this Valkyrie knows all that has happened in the nine worlds which, according to early Germanic thought, constituted the universe. He then asks that she teach him wisdom. The Valkyrie gives the hero a drink that contains special charms and spells, and then she gives him the runes of gladness. The Valkyrie then proceeds to tell the youth of no less than seven runes which were hers as a divine being. The fifth rune tells of the magic of healing by means of a tree. A single stanza in *The Poetic Edda* clearly states the power of these runes:

> Branch runes learn, if a healer you would be,
> And the cure for wounds you would work;
> On the bark you shall write, and on trees that are
> With boughs that to the east are bent.

The verses of this stanza reflect the belief that if this rune were properly 'worked' and the mark that identified it were then carved into the bark of a tree, the wound would be transferred to the tree and the injured party would be healed.

The regard, the esteem, and from time to time the fear, that the ancient Teutonic culture held for trees was not restricted to trees in a generic sense. The Eddic literature makes numerous references to specific kinds of trees that played some role in the societal life of the people. The *fir* tree, for example, was the tree under which a fay sat, giving rewards to the innocent and plaguing those who were guilty. Another tree that *The Poetic Edda* calls by name is the *yew*, whose wood was regularly used in the making of bows in the Nordic region (and in England), and the tree that gave its name to Ydalir ("Yew Dales"), the place where Ull -- the God of Archers -- had his hall. In addition to its use as the name of the first woman of the universe, the *elm* also was as a synonym for *mankind*. Also named in the Eddic literature is the *birch* whose blossoms were used in a drink that produced forgetfulness. One of the most frequently named trees is the *oak* which, because of its strength, was associated with the god Donner. It was under the oak tree that Donner and Loge once sought shelter. It was the tree whose bark cured illness, the tree whose acorns were used in a drink of forgetfulness, and the tree whose twigs and branches were used in fertility rites. It was the noble oak that was the most sacred tree in Teutondom and the tree whose wood was used to build the pyre on which the slain Siegfried would be placed. There are yet other trees that are named in Eddic poetry, such trees as the *hazel*, the *rose*, the *aspen*, the *beech*, and the *rowan*. Each of these last-named trees receives some special attention in the literature, and, for any of a number of reasons, almost pious consideration.

Wagner's lengthy study of the myths and legends of the Teutonic past had made him keenly aware of the fundamental importance of the forest environment that prevailed within that society's beliefs. He realized that nature essentially had dominated Teutonic life and that it was an integral aspect of that life's thought, rite, and ritual. It is not unusual, then, that he set much of his *Ring* drama within the wilds of nature, a nature that was replete with the hills, crags, valleys, rivers, and caves that are associated with forest terrain. The stage settings of four of the ten acts of the *Ring* include a forest as part of the scene, and one set of stage instructions even specifies that the forest be one of *fir* trees. (The word that Wagner used was *Tannewald* which, in modern German, is a poetic term that is usually interpreted as *pine woods*. The prefix of this compound, however, also means *fir*, and students of the *Ring* are often divided in their translation into English of the word. It would seem that the correct translation of Wagner's word is *fir wood* because, in addition to the composer's thorough familiarity with the mythical literature, the *pine* is not one of the trees that is featured in Eddic poetry.)

In addition to the fir tree, Wagner wove into his drama two other species of trees. One of these trees was the *linden*, and the other was the most sacrosanct, the most venerated, the holiest tree of all Teutondom, the *ash*.

The linden tree is one of the most popular trees in Germany. It is not mentioned in either of the *Eddas*, but it is heralded in German song, story, and folklore in general. In the numerous tales that feature the linden, it is the tree whose wood, when made into a cradle, will allow a first-child to perform great deeds. It is also the tree whose blossoms emit a fragrance that brings on insensibility and stupification. Such powers make the linden the tree for lovers and those who wish to fall in love. And, that same fragrance that brings on a lover's stupification could cause a hero to fall into a deep sleep of enchantment. It was in this last-mentioned capacity that Wagner made the linden tree a part of his drama. It is in *Siegfried*, in the second act, that the hero lies beneath a linden tree, there to dream of what his father and mother were like, and to wish that he could understand the song that the Forest Bird sings to him.

Of the numerous trees that played important roles in the ancient Teutonic thought, the one that was held in more reverence and accorded more profound religious esteem and attention than all others was the *ash*. The veneration of the ash tree was a basic principal of early Teutonic thought and that veneration is to be found throughout the Germanic myths and legends not only frequently, but in several forms. One of the first forms of ritual attachment to the ash was its depiction as the "tree of war." In this culture that prized combat and even allowed a special heaven for its greatest warriors (Valhalla), the ash was treasured because of the warnings regarding war that it silently issued. It was believed, for example, that if a battle was to be fought near an ash tree that was tall enough to tether a horse, the army that would come to fight would be a mighty force and the ensuing conflict was destined to be a long one with many dead and wounded warriors. At the same time, warriors -- in their fanatic cult of Wotan, who was closely associated with the ash -- desired to do battle beneath this tree because it was believed that if they were slain in such a spot, there would then be greater possibilities that the god would select them to join the elite ranks of his army in Valhalla. Another belief held that the howl of a wolf that was sitting beneath an ash was an indication that the time was favorable for waging war. Yet another war-related belief held that it was an ill-omen for a wounded warrior who was returning from battle to see an eagle sitting in the branches of an ash tree. Since eagles ate carrion, such a sight meant that the warrior would soon die. And, there was yet one more belief that caused the early Teutonic people to look upon the ash as a "tree of war," a belief that in some ways was of greater import than all others: To this war-oriented culture, the most valued weapon of war was the spear and the finest of all spears were made of the wood of the ash tree!

Wagner's study of the Teutonic myths had made him aware of the importance of the ash tree in the heathen culture. He brought that knowledge into his *Ring* drama by incorporating into the argument not one, but three ash trees! Each of these ashes appears separately, in different scenes of the music-drama, and each functions in a mythical manner that accommodates the respective dramatic situation.

One of this trio of ash trees appears more by reference than as an obvious part of the setting. The psychological impact that is created by the mention of this ash is, however, in its own way as impressive as the physical appearance of its two companion trees. The reference occurs in the final moments of the first act of *Siegfried*, shortly after the young Volsung learns that Mime possesses the two pieces of the sword that once belonged to his father. Eager to have the sword in order that he may face Fafner the Dragon and thus possibly learn the meaning of fear, Siegfried begins to reforge the sword himself. As he stands at the hearth and pumps the bellows, the youth tells of the ash that he felled and out of which he made the fuel that feeds the fire. He remarks how fiercely the wood burns, and he tells of the fire's brightness and its darting sparks. Siegfried's few words may be regarded by some readers as unnecessary thematic detail, but their importance becomes quite apparent when one realizes the significance of the ash in Teutonic thought, and that this is the most revered, the holiest of trees in all of Teutondom. This import is enhanced further when it is noted that this ash-fire that burns so intently will allow the great sword to be remade and that while this is the sword that will kill the Dragon, this is also the sword that will shatter the spear of authority with which the supreme god Wotan rules the universe! The subtle inference carried by Siegfried's words is dramatic, indeed remarkable, and if that subtlety is overshadowed by the dramatic and musical power of the scene, the use here of ash as firewood is a clear demonstration not only of Wagner's knowledge of Teutonic mythical matters, but also of the care and attention that he gave to even the most minute of details.

A second of the ashes is that impressive tree that dominates the first act of *Die Walküre*. Reference is made, of course, to that tree that comes up through the floor in Hunding's dwelling, rises, and then extends through the roof. The inclusion of this tree as a part of the stage arrangement was not the result of any desire on Wagner's part to create an unusual theatrical decor. Rather, this ash is not only vital to the development of the *Ring* story, but it is also an adaptation that Wagner made of a similar tree that is famed in German legend and myth. Wagner drew his inspiration for Hunding's tree from the *Branstock*, the name in the *Volsungasaga* of the giant oak that grew in King Volsung's main hall. As in the saga, so too in the *Ring* does the tree become the tree into whose trunk a mysterious stranger thrusts a sword, a sword that will be the best of swords for him who can withdraw it.

Wagner considered the Branstock to be a property whose legendary function accommodated itself most appropriately to the thematic development of his version of the Siegmund-Sieglinde story. However, as he transferred the tree from Volsung's hall to Hunding's dwelling, he also chose to make certain changes in the picture that the saga had presented. First, he determined that he would not allow his tree to have a name, probably because he did not wish to have any dramatic infringement on or detraction from that tree in his tale which was to dominate all the universe and which bore the name of World Ash. Secondly, as he brought the tree from the saga into his drama, he changed Volsung's *oak* to an *ash*. This change of species was not a capricious act on Wagner's part, as well it would seem at first glance. Rather, the change came about because of the composer's keen sense of both dramatic unity and dramatic continuity. Wagner was familiar with the Teutonic beliefs that related the oak tree with the god Donner. By converting Hunding's tree to an ash, he felt that he was removing, psychologically at least, that association with Donner, an association for which there was no dramatic need in his argument. At the same time, Wagner was cognizant of the fact that the stranger who had embedded a sword in its trunk was really Wotan. Thus, in converting the tree from an oak to an ash, Wagner was essentially establishing a relationship between that tree and the supreme god, a connection that would be made quite apparent later in his dreams, and one which also had a precedent in mythical belief.

The third of the ash trees of Wagner's *Ring* is one that has already been mentioned, the World Ash. This tree is not only the most prominent tree of Wagner's drama, it is the most prominent and the most important tree in all of Teutonic thought. The World Ash was the holiest of Teutondom's trees and for the early Teutonic peoples it was the symbol of the universe as well as the symbol of life itself.

In Old Norse the full and correct name for the great tree of Teutondom was *Askr Yggdrasil* which frequently was reduced to *Yggdrasil*. The word *askr* is translated as "ash" in English and "Esche" in German. The word *Yggdrasil* is a compound of two words that meant literally "the steed of Ygg." Thus, *Askr Yggdrasil* carried the rather awkward translation of "The Ash Steed of Ygg." The word "Ygg" was at once a common noun that meant "the terrible" or "the terrible one" and also a proper noun that was used as one of the many names of Wotan. Thus, *Askr Yggdrasil* can be translated in two additional ways: "The Ash Steed of the Terrible One" and "The Ash Steed of Wotan." In his *Ring*, Wagner regularly used only German names for his figures and properties, a procedure that eliminated the use of the Norse terms for the tree. Wagner's plan in this regard presented no difficulty as he merely put into German the most popular of names by which the tree was known, a name which was also the most frequently used in the mythical literature: *Welt-Esche* ("World Ash").

The World Ash Tree may well be the single most significant feature of all the Teutonic mythical concepts, at least if such import is adjudged by the quantity of related information that is to be found in Eddic literature. This ash was called "the best of trees," "the windy tree," "the high reaching tree," and Eddic verse also refers to the World Ash as "... the tree that casts abroad/Its limbs o'er every land." The inference in these verses is to Yggdrasil as the shelterer and protector of each of the nine worlds of the universe that were housed within its branches and at its roots and in which all life -- divine, supernatural, and mortal -- was sustained.

Yggdrasil was, in the minds of the ancient Teutonic people, the tree that represented life, and the life that it projected was a reflection of itself, defective and imperfect. Four creatures that resided in the tree presented a situation that has been interpreted as representative of the strife and tension that exists throughout the world. This depiction shows Vedrfolnir ("Weather-Bleached"), the hawk, sitting between the eyes of an eagle, and the serpent Nidhogg ("The Dark-Biter") gnawing the roots of the tree. A squirrel, Ratatosk ("The Swift Tusked") runs up and down the trunk of the tree between the two, each time carrying abusive messages. The destructive forces in life are symbolized by four harts that munch away at Yggdrasil's twigs. (Two of these harts have names that are also those of two of the first dwarfs that are created by the gods.) The same destructive forces are thought to be at work as the goat Heidrun feeds upon the leaves of Ljeradr, a tree located near Valhalla which scholars have long presumed to be the upper boughs of the World Ash Tree. (Heidrun was the animal that daily gave the clear mead that was the drink of the slain heroes who inhabited the celestial paradise of selected warriors.) Another hart, Eikdyrnir ("The Oak-Thorned"), from whose horn flowed a stream that fell into the spring Hvergelmir ("Cauldron Roaring") out of which all rivers came, also ate the leaves of Ljeradr. The damage that was caused by the serpent that gnawed at Yggdrasil's roots, and the harm brought on by the several harts that ate its leaves, wasted and weakened the great tree, and in the din of The Final Battle that would take place at the time of the destruction of the universe (*ragnarök**), the once mighty World Ash Tree would shake and tremble. Thus, despite the World Ash's status as the tree of all Teutonic life, despite its revered dominance over all trees in that culture, Yggdrasil's existence in the heathen fatalistic scheme of things was tenuous, destined to end in the final doom that was to overwhelm the universe.

There were yet other aspects of the mythical ash tree of the Germanic world that were related to the matters of life. At its base there was a dwelling that housed the three *Nornir* ("Norns") whose names were Urd, Verdandi, and Skull. These figures were the embodiments of fate, and renowned for their wisdom. It was this trio of sisters that determined the destiny of each man at his birth, and then carved the runes* of that fate into the roots or on the trunk of Yggdrasil.

The World Ash Tree had three roots, each of which housed some form of life. Eddic poetry states that Hel, the Guardian of the Dead, lived beneath the first root and that the Frost-Giants had their home beneath the second root. This same poetry records that the third root stretched through Midgard, the world of man.

The Prose Edda is not only more detailed in its depiction of Yggdrasil, but it also presents a different picture of the tree's roots. According to this work, the first root of the World Ash Tree extended into Asgard, the world of the gods, while the second root lay in the land of the Frost-Giants, where -- before time existed -- there was the great void of the universe, Ginnungagap ("Yawning Gap"). This *Edda* records that also under the second root of the ash lay Mimir's Spring, the spring whose waters contained the wisdom and understanding of the universe. Mimir was a water-spirit who drank the water of his spring out of the horn Gjall, and to whom Wotan once gave an eye as payment for a drink of these waters of knowledge. (The significance in Teutonic thought of Mimir is reflected in the fact that the World Ash Tree, on occasion, was called *Mimameid*, or "Mimir's Tree.") The Eddic prose then states that the third root of Yggdrasil extended over Niflheim, Land of the Dead, and the author continues by writing that it was under this third root that the spring Hvergelmir was located, and there also that the serpent Nidhogg gnawed at the tree. There was yet another spring to be found under the third root of the World Ash. This spring, whose waters were sacred, was guarded over by Urd, the Norn, and her two sisters. Each day the Norns sprinkled Yggdrasil with water from the spring, water which then became the dew that covered the world. The water of Urd's spring had its own magic in that everything that it touched became as white as the inner-skin of the shell of an egg. There were two birds that lived in this spring; they were called *swans*, and it was from this pair that all birds of this name came. It was at Urd's spring that the gods met every day to consult, to hold their court of justice, and to make decisions regarding all that was to happen in the world. To reach their meeting place, the gods rode their steeds across Bifrost, the Rainbow Bridge.

Yggdrasil, the World Ash Tree, the tree of life, the tree of fate, the tree of doom and destruction, was figuratively the center of the universe in the minds of the ancient Teutonic peoples. Wotan, the Supreme God, the Allfather, the Heerfather, was the principal god of Teutondom, the god most to be venerated and at the same time to be feared, the most powerful of all the forces of the universe. Thus, there is nothing of greater import and of more significance than the event that brings this tree and the god Wotan into a relationship that symbolizes the union of these two principal powers of Teutonic thought. This consequential incident occurs in a series of three stanzas in the Eddic poem "Hovamol" ("Ballad of the High One"). It is in these verses that Wotan is united with the tree which, in its own way, allowed that his authority as the supreme deity and the Allfather of the universe be strengthened and made greater through acquisition of the wisdom of the world. In the first of these verses, Wotan weens that he has hung from the branches of Yggdrasil. As he hung, head down, he wounded himself with his spear, Gungnir, a sacrifice of himself to himself. Wotan hung from the tree for nine nights. (*Nine* was the charmed number in Teutonic thought, and *time* in the early Germanic world was measured in *nights* rather than in *days* as is the modern custom.) No one offered food to the god; no one offered him drink. Then Wotan looked to the ground, and there beneath him he saw the runes*. Shrieking, he took them up, and wisdom came to the god. The knowledge that now was a part of the god was good and, as the verses state, he began to thrive and he grew, and was well. The poetry then records that each word or charm that Wotan uttered led him to another charm, and each act that he accomplished led him on to new acts.

The episode in which the god gains the treasured secrets of the runes* while he is joined to the World Ash vividly presents the Teutonic concept of the fusion of the dominant active and passive forces in the universe. Together, Wotan and the World Ash Tree are the world forces that generate, sustain, and control all that exists. This pair now becomes a symbol of both universal life and death, a symbol for a glorious life after death, and equally so, a stimulus *to be*. (Over the years numerous scholars have found in the incident of Wotan and Yggdrasil the antecedent to an episode of recognized importance in later Christian belief, the Crucifixion of Christ.)

There can be no doubt that Yggdrasil was the central belief around which the early Germanics developed their total thought and then allowed it to flourish. Its form was that of a tree, an object that was native and natural to these people whose culture was essentially a forest culture. But the form of the World Ash appropriately accommodated the concepts that were emerging. Such a situation was eagerly accepted by the people and a tree became something much more that a mere tree. This form was transformed; the tree remained a tree but it was now a transcendental experience that responded to the religious needs as the people envisioned them. Yggdrasil became the axis of life, the supporter of life that guarded the destiny of all things as that destiny had been engraved upon its trunk. Yggdrasil afforded a comfort in that it offered a unity in an otherwise unorganized, primitive life; Yggdrasil allowed a modicum of stability in an intellectually unsophisticated society; Yggdrasil furnished the responses that all cultures have sought to their inquiries into the matters of life and the nature that surrounded that life.

The Yggdrasil of *The Ring of the Nibelung*, or as Wagner called it, the World Ash ("Welt-Esche"), is essentially a dramatic counterpart of the original. Wagner's Ash figures prominently in the first part of the "Prelude" of *Götterdämmerung* where it stands in the darkness of night. Like its mythological inspiration, Wagner's World Ash casts an aura of transcendence that lies beyond the realm of normal existence. One senses that it was a mighty tree, a powerful tree, a tree that even now casts off a certain majesty, a tree that seems to have no peer for it is truly the tree of all life. And, as in the myths, so too do the Norns of the *Ring* meet at the tree's base, there to determine the fate of the world and all that reside in that world. Unlike the Norns of the myths, Wagner's sisters do not carve the runes of the fate of all living things on the trunk of the World Ash, but rather they weave that fate into their Cord of Destiny, a property that Wagner created for his drama.

Wagner also chose to create his own names for the Norns of the *Ring*. He preferred numbers, that is First, Second, and Third, rather than names, probably because in the beginning there was only one Germanic Norn (Urd), the other two coming into existence after the introduction into Teutonic culture of the trio of classical Fates. Wagner's Norns gather at the base of the tree to recall the days of Wotan's rule, to tell of the initiation of the god's decline, and then to foretell of the cataclysm that soon is to befall the world. As the Norns weave their Cord of Destiny, they also tell of a spring that flows at the foot of the *Ring's* World Ash, a spring whose waters, much like those of the mythological Mimir's Spring, whispered the wisdom of the world, and a spring from which Wotan once drank and gave an eye as payment.

Wagner's Ash, like Yggdrasil, was once a lush, green, vital tree. Now, its strength is gone. If the harts had nibbled at Yggdrasil and Nidhogg had gnawed into its trunk, thus weakening the tree, the deterioration of Wagner's Ash Tree began when Wotan tore from it a branch from which his spear of authority was to be fashioned, the spear on which the runes* of the god's rule were carved. The wound that Wotan had caused gravely injured the tree and it began to grow weak. In time, the wound became worse, and soon blight invaded the trunk and branches. Then, the Spring of Wisdom that bubbled at the tree's base dried away and the World Ash of the *Ring* died. Now, it could no longer accept within its branches the Cord of Destiny that the Norns fashioned as they wove and they sang. The ravages that plagued the Tree of Teutondom and those that brought on the slow demise of Wagner's World Ash are distinct, but in each situation they are symbols as well as reflections of the decay that ancient Teutonic thought believed eroded the world, the persistent disintegration that signals the ultimate destruction of all things.

The absolute ends of each of the two World Ash Trees, that final time when the trees are no more, are, like the causes of each tree's situation in the universe, uniquely different. The Tree of Teutondom has withstood the many violences that life has placed upon it, but when the moment arrives that the gods band together, draw upon the army in Valhalla, and march out to do battle with their enemies, there can be no doubt as to the fate of the Tree. As the clash of arms signals The Final Battle*, the last conflict before the world will see its end, the Eddic literature tells us that the great Tree sways and shakes and trembles, and the inference is, of course, that it too will be consumed, just as will all else in the universe. Wagner knew that his World Ash Tree must stand in the universe like its mythological prototype, but his sense of the dramatic, his sense of theater, allowed him to conceive of a final end that replaced the passive role of the Eddic Ash, an end that would let his Tree have a bold, active role in the *ragnarök** that he had devised for his lengthy drama. In that last scene of the music-drama, Wotan is aware that his acts of an earlier time cannot now be undone and that these acts have brought to him and the universe the fate of total doom. Wagner's gods, however, do not go into battle as they did in mythical beliefs. Rather, the Allfather orders that the World Ash be felled and that its boughs be placed around Valhalla where he has gathered the gods of Teutondom to await the flames that will set it ablaze. As Wagner planned it, the hero Siegfried will be slain by Hagen and his body placed on a great pyre. Brünnhilde will proclaim the hero to the world, and then set the pyre ablaze. The fire from Siegfried's pyre will consume the corrupt world that the gods have made and the flames will then rise toward the heavens. At the same time, the gods learn from Wotan's ravens what has transpired on earth and Wotan, as the Norns had foretold, picks up the point of his splintered spear, thrusts it into the breast of Loge, the fire-god, and sets afire the boughs of the World Ash Tree and in the conflagration that ensues the deities will be brought to their destruction.

The World Ash Tree is but one of a myriad of mythical concerns that Wagner selectively but adeptly wove into his argument of *The Ring of the Nibelung*. Wagner's Ash tree, and the dramatic role he gave it, reveal not only the composer's intimate familiarity with the myths and legends of his culture's past, but also his recognition, and more importantly his understanding, of the profound influence such matters had on the lives of the people of that early society. It is obvious that Wagner made certain adaptations to accommodate the original Yggdrasil to his own thematic needs. However, as he transferred the tree and its details from mythical thought and Eddic literature to his operatic libretto, he never altered the essence of the fundamental significance of the Tree, and he kept sacred its stature as the ancient Teutonic symbol of the universe.

Curiously, it was more by accident than by initial design that the World Ash Tree came to be a part of the *Ring*. In late October, 1848, Wagner completed the preliminaries of a poem that he titled *Siegfrieds Tod*, a title that he would change later to *Götterdämmerung*. (At the time, Wagner had not yet begun work on any of the other three dramas.) The poem at hand was a drama of three acts, the first of which opened upon the Hall of the Gibichungs. A librettist friend, one in whom Wagner had firm confidence, studied the work and indicated that he felt that the two principal themes of the drama were insufficiently developed. Those two themes were the dilemma in which Wotan found himself and the relationship of Siegfried and Brünnhilde. Wagner's friend suggested that if an audience was to understand these matters completely, and thus to feel their dramatic impact, additional material was needed. Wagner himself had sensed a certain incompleteness in his work, and prodded by his friend's advice, he acted immediately on the suggestion. Rather than change radically the body of the work, and therefore be forced to rewrite the three acts already completed, Wagner decided to add a 'fore-scene,' a "Prelude" that would address itself to the concerns expressed by his friend. Wagner needed only a few days to complete his "Vorspiel," a matter of two separate scenes. In one of these scenes he elaborated on the impassioned relationship of the young Volsung and the banished Valkyrie. In the other scene, which would open the opera, Wagner placed the three Norns at the base of the World Ash and caused them to recount the story of Wotan and the World Ash tree. Thus it was that Yggdrasil, Wagner's "Welt-Esche," the World Ash Tree, became an integral part of the landmark work that so changed the concepts of drama and music.

III
THE RAINBOW BRIDGE

One of the most striking musico-dramatic scenes in the *Ring*, and indeed in all of musico-dramatic art, occurs during the final moments of *Das Rheingold*. After the giant Fafner has slain his brother Fasolt and has departed with the payment of tainted gold given to the pair by the gods for their labors on Valhalla, Fricka informs her husband that the mighty fortress is now his, that it now awaits the Supreme God of Teutondom. Donner waves his famed hammer, points it toward the skies, and then causes its magic to bring about a great storm to clear away the mists that hide the celestial castle from view. As the lightning and thunder abate, and the clouds disperse, Froh slowly waves his arm and causes a majestic rainbow to appear. Its arc rises high in the heavens as it spans the space between the noble fortress and the mountain heights on which the gods are standing. It is the Rainbow Bridge (*Regenbogenbrücke*), the bridge over which Wotan will lead the gods as they make their first entrance into Valhalla.

Wagner's use of the rainbow as a pathway by which the gods enter and exit their divine world is an accurate dramatic duplication of one of the most distinctive concepts of early Teutonic thought. In the beliefs of the early Germanic peoples, the rainbow was a celestial bridge that was exclusive to the gods, much in the manner that the Milky Way -- known to these early people as *Wotan's Way's* -- was viewed as the gods' celestial roadway.

Eddic literature frequently cites the rainbow bridge by its name. It is called *Bifrost*, occasionally *Bilrost*. This Old Norse name can be translated into English as "Quivering Roadway," with the words "Tremulous" and "Pathway" as acceptable substitutes. This same literature refers to Bifrost as *Asabru*, that is, "Bridge of the Aesir Gods." ("Aesir" is the name of the clan of gods of which Wotan is the head god. A clan of lesser gods is the *Vanir* or "Wanes.") This celebrated bridge is also known as "the road to Wotan's realm," and naturally, Bifrost is considered to be "the best of bridges."

The early people of Teutondom viewed Bifrost as a very special bridge, one which they held in the highest regard. For these people Bifrost was the means by which the gods made their frequent journeys to the other worlds of the universe*. The early Germanics also believed that Bifrost was used daily by the gods when they crossed it to reach the World Ash Tree where they held their councils and made their decisions regarding matters of the world that came before them. This divine aura that was associated with Bifrost distinguished it as one of the most respected items of all Teutonic thought, so esteemed, in fact, that it was one of the few items on which the runes of wisdom, knowledge, and conduct could be engraved. (Wotan's spear was another item on which the runes could be inscribed.)

Bifrost was a strong bridge. The gods had built it, and as they worked they applied their divine skills and ingenuity. The Eddic literature states that Bifrost was made of three different kinds of materials, each of a distinct color. That literature also tells us that the *red* of Bifrost was "fire," but those same writings are silent regarding the two other materials and the color of each!

Despite the great strength that had been built into it, Bifrost was not a structure that was destined to endure forever. The bridge of Teutondom was fated, as was almost everything in the heathen Teutonic universe, to a final end, the same doom and destruction that was to befall the gods. And, curiously, Bifrost was to have a role in its own downfall. As the Eddic verses tell the tale, Surt would lead his army of Fire-Giants out of their home in Muspellsheim, Land of Fire, make his way northward until he and his warriors came to Bifrost which they then crossed in order to meet the gods in The Final Battle*. As the great army made its way across the bridge of Teutondom, the weight of the warriors began to weaken it. In time, as the flames of the Fire-Giants leaped about, Bifrost began to shake, to tremble, and then to break apart. During this last battle of the universe, Bifrost would become enveloped in flames, and then collapse. Such was the end of the Rainbow Bridge in ancient Teutonic thought.

Bifrost was one of those items of Teutonic beliefs which, like others of significance, was associated with a single major Germanic god. Although the bridge had been built by the gods and was a part of the divine world that all the gods used and enjoyed, its protection, its welfare, and its guardianship were entrusted to one divine figure: That god so closely associated with Bifrost and its safety was Heimdall. Heimdall's divine title was "Watchman of the Gods" and it was his obligation to be ever-alert for the enemies of the gods who one day, according to the prophets, would attempt to destroy the gods of Teutondom. Heimdall was to warn the deities of any encroaching enemy who would have to use Bifrost to gain entrance to the Land of Gods. He took great care in fulfilling his obligation because he was aware of the prophesied attack that would be made upon the gods by Surt and the Fire-Giants.

The Eddic literature describes the Guardian of the Rainbow Bridge rather completely. Heimdall had been born of nine women who, according to *The Prose Edda*, were sisters. He was a god of great strength, an attribute that he had gained from the earth, from the sea, and from the blood of sacrificed swine. This popular god had other attributes that aided him in his guardianship of the famed bridge of Teutondom: he needed less sleep than a bird; he could see one hundred leagues by day or by night; his hearing was so sharp that he could hear the grass grow as well as the wool on a sheep.

As was common among the Teutonic gods, Heimdall had certain possessions of his own. The god had a sword whose name was "Head," and he rode a horse whose name was Gulltopp ("Gold Tuft"). Heimdall also had his own dwelling, as did most of the major Germanic gods. Heimdall's home was named Himinbjorg ("Cliff" or "Mount of Heaven") . This abode stood at that point where the Rainbow Bridge joined the Land of the Gods. It was from his dwelling that Heimdall kept watch over Bifrost. Special to the god was his horn Gjallarhorn ("Shrieking Horn"), whose sound could be heard around the world. This horn lay buried under the World Ash Tree and would be dug up and sounded by Heimdall to awaken the gods when Surt and his attacking army of Fire-Giants gave signs that they were going to cross Bifrost. Despite the precautions of the gods and despite Heimdall's continued alertness, the enemies of the gods attack and The Final Battle takes place. It is in this last struggle that the gods of Teutondom are destroyed and the battle in which Heimdall and Loge fight and -- in the end -- slay each other.

Heimdall, like the Allfather Wotan, was known by several names. The most significant of these was, of course, "Watchman of the Gods," but he was also frequently called the "White God." Scholars have interpreted this latter name as meaning that Heimdall was God of Light. That interpretation is possible because of the god's association with the rainbow and the sunlight necessary to make it appear. Another of Heimdall's many names was "Seeker of Freia's Necklace," and because of his struggle in The Final Battle with the cunning spirit of the Teutonic world, he was also called "Foe of Loge." There were yet other names that were given to this important god, names such as Vindler ("The Turner") and Hallinskidi ("Ram"), and because Heimdall had gold teeth, he was also known as Gullintanni ("Gold-Toothed").

Heimdall wandered at large, much like Wotan, and some of the god's adventures made their way into the ancient Germanic myths. Perhaps the most significant of these tales is that found in one of the Eddic poems titled "The Ballad of Rig." This poem recounts how Heimdall, now known as Rig ("King"), became celebrated throughout the mythical world as the father of three types of people: thralls, peasant farmers, and warriors.

Heimdall was, above all else, a gracious god. A faculty for inspiration as well as a kind of creative element can be discerned in his figure. Such traits, coupled with the sense of trust that he engendered and the overall repute and regard that he enjoyed, allowed him to be one of the most respected figures in Teutonic thought and beliefs. That respect was almost of a permanent nature because even today, especially in Norway, there are still to be found numerous places that bear the god's name.

Despite the mythical prominence that Heimdall enjoyed, and despite his mythical esteem, Heimdall never gained quite the renown of the other gods of Teutondom. And, Heimdall never knew the elevated godhood that came to Wotan, to Donner, and to Froh. It is entirely possible that Heimdall's godhood exhibited less brilliancy than that of other Teutonic deities, but such lesser divine status did not prohibit his relationship with one of Teutondom's most exalted concepts, the Rainbow Bridge. Such a situation has been an enigma to scholars who, even after extensive and profound studies of Teutondom's divine hierarchy, admit to a certain amount of bewilderment, if not confusion, regarding Heimdall's true divine status. The enigma has persisted to the present day.

Wagner excluded Heimdall from his *Ring* drama! As the composer arranged his dramatic gallery of gods according to his own scheme of things, he accepted the Rainbow Bridge, but he rejected its guardian, Heimdall. He could accept the theatrical qualities that the mythical Bifrost obviously offered, but its care and guardianship would go to Froh rather than to the White God. (Wagner's mythical plan seems to parallel another of his changes of mythical reality, the substitution of Freia for Idun as guardian of the Golden Apples.) Wagner's rearrangement of this mythical matter may be considered, at first glance, a radical alteration of the essence of the ancient myths. Yet, a more careful examination of Wagner's apparent reasons for his replacement of Heimdall with Froh reveals that the composer's thought, at least for theatrical purposes, was essentially sound.

There are several reasons that caused Wagner to place the charge of the Rainbow Bridge in Froh's hands. First and foremost, Froh was one of the most important of the Teutonic gods. Along with Wotan and Donner, he formed what is frequently referred to as the "Triad" of Germanic deities, and such a belief indicated that in certain ways he had a divine status equal to that of Wotan. It is mythological fact that in some parts of the Teutonic world, principally in Sweden, Froh was the supreme god over Wotan.

Froh was also a most beloved god. He brought about love, and fruitfulness, and abundance. Froh controlled the sunshine, which made his countenance shine brightly and which made him known as the God of Summer. Froh also controlled rain which, when combined with the sunshine, usually produced a rainbow. And, since rain and sunshine were imperative for the growth of foodstuffs, especially grain, Froh was also looked upon as a god of fertility of the soil and, therefore, he was frequently invoked at both planting and harvest time.

There can be no doubt about Froh's place in the divine world of the Teutonic peoples. He was venerated intensely on several distinct matters, and in every region of Teutondom. And, as stated before, that veneration was often greater than that afforded Wotan. An indication of the divine influence that Froh had with the early Teutonic people is evidenced in the fact that there is a definite relationship between this god's runic mark and the letter "F" of the modern alphabet. Indeed, Froh was a major factor in the religious thought that pervaded the ancient Germanic regions.

Froh's elevated position in heathen Germanic thought and belief was sufficient reason to include him in any tale of the gods. It can be said with rather certain assurance, however, that his appearance in such a story, in the company of such other gods as Wotan and Donner, was really a mythological necessity. Wagner knew his way about in the myths of his culture. His extensive studies of the Germanic past had made him aware of the Teutonic hierarchy of the gods and Froh obviously had to be a part of the divine authority that was to exist in his poem. Then, too, there was the added matter of the god's relationship with nature, that is, with rain, with sunshine, and with soil, which he could easily convert to his own dramatic benefit; Wagner would make Froh his God of the Fields. At the same time, Wagner realized that the Rainbow Bridge had emerged as a prime property in the development of his *Ring* story. He also knew that Heimdall, its Guardian, did not command the attention as did his God of the Fields and since he had already made some alterations in the character of his Froh, why not still others! After all, Froh was a god of nature and was not Bifrost a most notable phenomenon of nature's world! Thus, as with Freia and Idun, so with Froh and Heimdall, and the *Ring's* 'God of the Fields' became the Guardian of the Rainbow Bridge!

It is obvious that Wagner accepted the Teutonic concept of the Rainbow Bridge as well as its function in the divine world. It is equally apparent that he recognized the belief that this celebrated bridge merited a guardian, but he reverted to his own dramatic needs regarding the specific god who would serve as Bifrost's overseer. In a sense, he rejected the

Heimdall of the myths and supplied his Froh. Heimdall was not, however, all that was associated with Bifrost that Wagner put aside. He refused to use the Nordic name by which the bridge was known, and, since there was no equivalent name in German, he referred to Bifrost simply as "Rainbow Bridge"; he did not include in his poem any of the mythical beliefs that were concerned with its construction by the gods, and he excluded any mention of the materials that these gods used; and, finally, he had no need of the bridge in the ultimate destruction of the world as he had planned it.

Wagner's Rainbow Bridge appears but once in the *Ring* drama, and then only briefly, in *Das Rheingold*. This appearance of the bridge is more theatrical than thematic, that is, it is used functionally rather than as a pertinent contributor to the development of the theme. The bridge is to serve as a pathway for the gods as they make their way into Valhalla. Used in this manner, the Rainbow Bridge is an appropriate property for this drama whose *dramatis personae* consists entirely of supernatural beings and their supernatural properties. The use of the Rainbow Bridge in this manner is also mythically correct, as evidenced in the Eddic poetry and prose. Further, such use also serves as a tangible means that will serve Wagner well as he prepares the dramatic and imposing climax to this first part of the *Ring*. Indeed, Wagner, the astute student of his culture's past, worked the myths of his culture well, and Bifrost appears most naturally within the totally mythical framework of this drama whose argument is clothed entirely in concepts and beliefs that abounded in the early Germanic culture.

IV
DONNER'S HAMMER

It is possibly arguable but it is not unreasonable to assert that the most renowned, the most celebrated, the most famous article in the religious thought of the early Teutonic people was Donner's great hammer, Mjollnir. With the possible exception of Valhalla, this instrument, this magic tool is more widely known today outside of Teutonic geography than any other feature or aspect of ancient Germanic beliefs. This famed hammer was one of three articles that the God of Thunder possessed. One of the other articles was a pair of iron gloves with which he gripped the mighty Mjollnir and the third of this trio of possessions was a belt which, when worn, doubled the already substantial strength of the god.

Although it is Mjollnir that is celebrated in tales of the early Teutonic people, it really is the second of two hammers that Donner possessed. The god's first hammer was a stone implement that had been broken by a sword that Thjasse the giant had forged and with which he intended to destroy the world of the gods. However, Thjasse is surprised in his sleep by Mimir who puts the giant in chains and flees with the sword. Svipdag, a hero, seeks out the sword and in a battle with Halfdan, son of Donner, he cleaves the god's hammer, rendering it useless. This implement then fades into mythical oblivion.

Mjollnir, which translates into English as "Mauler" or "Crusher," or perhaps "Destroyer," was hardly the tool that is brought to mind by modern usage of the word 'hammer.' The use of that word, both in English and in

German, to refer to Donner's prized possession is a linguistic result of the ancient use of the Old Norse word *hamarr* (OHG - *hamar*; OE - *hamor*; ME - *hamer*) which originally denoted "hard stone" or "rock," in the sense of "crag." As stone began to be used as implements or tools, that piece of stone that was used 'to pound' or 'to strike' acquired the generic name *hamarr*. Mjollnir was not made of stone, but its uses seemed to conform with those of the early *hamarr*, and the term thus became permanently associated with this divine article.

Eddic literature is rather detailed in its depiction of the origin of this treasured instrument. According to the story that is found in *The Prose Edda*, Donner's hammer was the masterwork of the smiths of the mythological world, the dwarfs, and was forged by two brothers who had set to work as a result of the machinations of the crafty Loge. The cunning and crafty spirit of the supernatural world had approached the dwarf Brokk and wagered that he and his brother, Eitri, could not produce three articles as fine as three items which the gods possessed and which they prized so highly.

The trio of articles to which Loge referred was three of the gods' most treasured possessions, items which had been made by certain other dwarfs. One of these wondrous articles was the hair that was made of gold and which grew like normal hair on the head of Sif, Donner's wife. Second of these prized items was Froh's marvelous ship Skidbladnir ("Wooden-Bladed") which always collected a breeze when it sailed and which could be folded and carried about in a pocket. The third article that was valued so highly was Wotan's spear, Gungnir, which always granted victory in battle.

Brokk and Eitri accepted Loge's wager and the pair set about immediately to win the bet. The two dwarfs planned their operation very carefully: Brokk would work the bellows which he would pump without any interruption in order that the fire would always burn at its hottest, and Eitri would forge the three pieces. The skin of a pig was then placed in the furnace. After the skin had been heated to the proper temperature, Eitri took it from the furnace and fashioned Guillinbursti ("Gold-Bristle"), a boar that could run over water and through the air faster than a horse. This boar, which had bristles of gold, was given to Froh. During the heating of the pigskin, a fly had lighted on Brokk's hand and had stung him. Despite this annoyance, the dwarf had not interrupted his work at the bellows. Eitri then put gold into the furnace and cautioned his brother that the bellows should not be slowed in the slightest during the smelting of the precious metal. As Brokk worked the bellows, the fly returned, and again stung him, this time on the neck and twice as hard as the first sting. The dwarf was very much disturbed by what had happened, but he did not stop his work. This time, Eitri was able to fashion the ring Draupnir ("Dropper"), from which eight rings of gold would drop every ninth night. Draupnir became the property of Wotan. Eitri then placed some iron-ore into the furnace, after which he warned his brother that the bellows must be pumped without interruption, that if he stopped, the treasure on which they worked would be ruined. Eitri then left while Brokk feverishly pumped the bellows. But, as before, the fly returned and this time it buzzed around Brokk's head. Brokk continued his work. Finally, the fly landed between Brokk's eyes, and stung the dwarf on an eyelid. The bite of the fly drew blood, enough blood that it ran in a stream down Brokk's face and into his eye. The dwarf was temporarily blinded, and he stopped the bellows just long enough to raise a hand to frighten away the fly and then to rub his painful eye. Eitri returned at that moment and immediately went to the furnace to inspect the metal. He told Brokk that the pause in the working of the bellows had almost ruined the iron. Eitri then withdrew the metal from the furnace and forged the item. This treasure was Mjollnir, the hammer that became Donner's property. Eitri had worked well, but despite his skill as a smith, the hammer had one flaw: The handle was quite short!

The tale of Mjollnir's origin ends with the statement that the hammer has a very short handle. The inference conveyed by the tale and its abrupt ending is that Mjollnir's short handle was the result of Brokk's stopping the forging process in order to chase away the fly, a pause that prohibited the completion of a total item. That inference is contradicted in a later Eddic writing which tells how Donner, in one of his many battles, threw his hammer and it broke when it struck a mountainous rock. This latter version of how the handle of Mjollnir became so short is, in the main, discounted in favor of the version found in the tale of Brokk and his brother.

The import and significance in heathen Teutonic thought of Donner's hammer is evidenced in several different ways, not the least of which is the inclusion in *The Poetic Edda* of a poem of thirty-three stanzas in which Mjollnir is essentially the protagonist. The poem is "Thrymsvida" ("The Lay of Thrym"), one of the most famous of all Eddic poems. The verses of this Eddic writing tell of the theft of the famous hammer by a Frost-Giant, Thrym, who hid it deep in the earth and then stated that he would return it only if he were given the goddess Freia as a wife. The gods were quite upset at the loss of the hammer. Their concern became so great that they met in council under the World Ash Tree to discuss how their treasure might be rescued. Ultimately, Donner -- aided by Loge -- retrieved Mjollnir with which the god then slew Thrym and, as the verses state, "...all the folks of the giants."

Donner's use of Mjollnir to slay Thrym and the other giants associated with him is but one of numerous incidents in which one of the several uses of the hammer is on view. Mjollnir was, above all else, a formidable weapon. It was strong, it was powerful, powerful enough to cut deep valleys in mountains when it was thrown. And, when Donner threw the hammer, it always hit its mark and then returned to the god's hand. Donner carried Mjollnir with him at all times as he traveled about the universe exercising his enormous capacity for adventure and combat. The god used the hammer to vent upon others the explosive wrath that was so much a part of his nature, and Mjollnir became his principal means of defense in the many confrontations that he had, especially those that he had with the enemies of the gods, the giants. On one occasion, Donner used the hammer to shatter the stone head of the giant Hrungnir; on another of his journeys the god struck the giant Skrymir three times with Mjollnir; on yet another trip, this time out to sea, Donner confronted Jormungander, the serpent whose body encircled the earth, and the god threw his hammer at the monster. Donner's use of Mjollnir as a weapon was not restricted to giants and monsters. He once used the hammer to threaten the mischievous Loge who had been revealing certain intimate details about the private behavior of the gods. And once he raised Mjollnir against Wotan, the King of the Gods, who -- at the time -- was in one of his many guises, this time as Harbard ("Grey

Beard"). There were, however, some times when Mjollnir was not in use, and then it could be made so small that it could be placed in the god's shirt.

There was another feature or attribute of Mjollnir that became a permanent and lasting belief in Teutonic culture. Early Germanic thought held that Donner's hammer was responsible for thunder and lightning. This heathen thought believed that Donner frequently sped through the heavens in his goat-drawn chariot. Often, when the god made such journeys, he had been enraged by some matter. When the god bristled in anger, he would use his great strength to throw his hammer from the speeding chariot. On such occasions, Mjollnir traveled with such speed that it rented the skies and caused the clouds to rumble loudly. When the hammer hit its mark, it struck with such force that it created a great spark of fire and caused a deafening noise. The spark was lightning and the noise was thunder. (Some mythologists have advanced the hypothesis that Mjollnir also carried a special mark, and when the hammer struck its target it left an imprint of the mark: That mark was the swastika.)

The belief that Donner and Mjollnir created the two powerful forces of nature, lightning and thunder, was prevalent throughout all of Teutondom. An associated belief, also widespread in the Germanic world, held that the absence of lightning and thunder during the period of winter was caused by the theft of Donner's hammer and its removal for a time from the world by the Frost-Giant Thrym. Such concepts persisted well into the eighteenth century and some remnants of these beliefs continue to circulate today in many parts of the world. The association of Donner with thunder and lightning was so widespread and so ingrained into the culture that the German language adopted the god's name as the word for "thunder," and even accepted a related word *Donnerschlag*, meaning "thunderbolt." (A similar situation exists in the English language in which the word *thunder* is derived from the name *Thor*, which was Donner's name in the Scandinavian area of Teutondom.)

The authority that Mjollnir had, that is as the 'mauler' or 'destroyer' that its name denotes, and those powers that allowed it to create thunder and lightning were but part of the magic that the heathen Teutonic mind had invested in Donner's hammer. In addition to these relatively outward and demonstrative forces, Mjollnir also possessed a unique, singular quality, a divine-like strength that elevated it to a status far above that regularly enjoyed by other articles that were the property of the gods. In a word, Mjollnir was the instrument of consecration as well as resurrection! These powers are evidenced in Eddic literature in separate incidents. On one occasion Donner stands before the pyre on which lie's the body of Balder, the most beloved god of Teutondom, and that of his wife Nanna, both of which are awaiting cremation. The god solemnly raises Mjollnir in the act of consecration. It is at this point that two versions continue the episode. One version continues with the cremation as it had been planned, while another version tells of Balder's immediate resurrection. Regardless of the specific endings of these tales, Balder is raised at some time, and returns to the world after the doom and destruction of *ragnarök**. In this new life, Balder occupies the fortress Valhalla and becomes the symbol of a new world of peace. On another occasion, Donner and Loge are on a journey. The pair had traveled all day, and in the evening, as the meal-hour approached, the god proceeded to slaughter the goats that pulled his chariot, after which they were prepared and served as food. The next morning, as Donner and Loge prepare to continue their journey, the god approaches the skins and bones of the animals. Standing beside the carcasses, Donner raises Mjollnir above the animals' remains and, in an instance, the goats are raised, brought back to life, once again ready to pull his chariot through the heavens.

The several magical qualities that were associated with Mjollnir caused it to be at once an object of awe, an instrument to be feared, an article to be revered in wonder, and an item to be respected most intensely. The hammer's place within the early Teutonic religious thought was both commanding and permanent. However, perhaps the most important, if not the most significant, aspect of Mjollnir's existence is not any of the magical feats that it performed but rather the fact that it was the only prominent divine article that would survive the cataclysmic end that was to be inflicted upon the world, the *ragnarök** that would one day engulf the gods and their universe. As the story is told in *The Poetic Edda*, Mjollnir endured the long, cold winter that preceded the final destruction. Then, as the Fire-Giants crossed the Rainbow Bridge and the monsters of the world gathered to confront the gods in The Final Battle*, Donner took up his great weapon and prepared himself for combat in the ultimate struggle. Donner fought Midgardsorm, the World Serpent, and slew him with his hammer. But, as the god walked away from the body of the monster-child of Loge, he fell dead, killed by the poisonous slaver that the serpent had drooled upon him. As the other gods die, and the world is overcome by fire and flood, Mjollnir remains untouched, unharmed, and undamaged. The famed hammer survives the old order and emerges in the new, this time coming into the hands of Donner's sons Magni ("Might") and Modi ("Wrath"), where it was to remain.

The same concepts that had given rise to a new universe, one governed by righteous gods and freed from the ills and evils of corruption, also occasioned new cultural beliefs regarding Mjollnir. The hammer continued to be the cause of lightning and thunder, but in this new world such natural phenomena were no longer viewed as omens of destruction and disaster. Now, the thunder and lightning that the hammer made were, in a narrow sense, associated with the growth of abundant crops, and in a broader sense welcome signs of good, symbols that guaranteed success to any undertaking that had been planned or scheduled. Mjollnir also retained its attributes of strength and power, but in its new existence it was no longer seen as a weapon, as the "lover of murder": In the world that had replaced the old, the hammer was a protector of the honest and the just. And, Mjollnir became the symbol of good, of plenty, and of security. The hammer was now invoked; brides sought its blessings; men turned to it for protection, and at the burial of righteous persons, the cadavers were consecrated with it. In the new life that Donner's hammer now enjoyed, it became a most sacred item, not unlike the Cross in Christian concepts.

The rank, the authority, the prominence, and indeed the significance in heathen Teutonic cultural thought of Donner's hammer never diminished through the years. Although unquestioned beliefs in the powers of Mjollnir slowly gave way to invading Christian concepts, the import of this hammer was not easily or quickly erased from the Teutonic mind. In the Middle Ages the hammer was still used to hallow the dead, and, in some regions, until the early part of the seventeenth century, the people continued to believe that Mjollnir could bring the dead back to life. Despite the dominance of

Christianity that was to spread over the Teutonic world, Donner's hammer retained its image as one of the most respected objects from an earlier world.

Wagner was well-acquainted with Mjollnir. His study of the ancient Germanic past, and his personal familiarity with later cultures had impressed upon him not only the prominence of Donner's hammer in Teutonic beliefs, but also its impact on societal and cultural thought and behavior. Eddic literature itself had convinced him that the god's hammer, like Wotan's spear, had been so significant a concept and its association with Donner had been so complete and thorough, that he could not omit it from any story in which the god was a part. At the same time, Wagner sensed that this hammer probably could not offer any serious thematic contribution to his tale of the gods and the activities that he had envisioned for them. As he juggled the entire matter of Mjollnir in his mind, and as he conceived the role that it would have in his drama, he saw the hammer as it was and as it had existed in the earliest of times. Slowly, Mjollnir's role began to evolve in Wagner's thoughts and when he arrived at that point in his poem where Donner was to make his appearance, the role of the hammer was fixed.

Wagner believed that the hammer of his *Ring* drama, which would remain nameless, should have two of the several functions that it had carried out in the Teutonic myths. It would, of course, be the property of the blustery god who would wield it as a mighty and powerful weapon and who would also use it to clear the skies and to bring about great claps of thunder and streaks of lightning that would pierce the heavens. Both of these uses occur in *Das Rheingold*, the only part of the *Ring* in which Donner and his hammer are to be found. The first use of the hammer comes early in the drama. Wotan has been attempting, with little success, to persuade the giants Fasolt and Fafner that they should accept some wage other than the goddess Freia who had been pledged to them as the reward for their labors on Valhalla. At one point in the discussion, Froh moves to protect Freia, and the giants step forward as if to keep her from the god. Donner, hammer in hand, quickly places himself between the two giants, his hammer raised in a threatening manner. The god then asks the brothers if they are aware that the might of his hammer has given many giants their due payment. The God of Thunder then adds that the giants' conduct in the matter at hand merits such a payment. The reference, of course, is to the hammer as a slayer of giants, a use to which the hammer was often put in mythical literature. The second use of the hammer comes later, after the matter of the payment to the giants has been settled. The gods of the universe prepare to make their initial entrance into the celestial fortress Valhalla, which now belongs to them. The castle is veiled from view by a dense mist. Donner mounts a large rock. He raises his hammer above his head and swings it toward the heavens. Slowly at first, but ever increasing the momentum of his hammer, Donner eyes the dark sky. Suddenly, he raises the hammer high above his head and brings it down with all his might. A great clap of thunder is heard as the hammer hits the rock, and a flash of lightning streaks through the sky. The foreboding clouds have vanished, the mist has been dispelled, and Valhalla can be seen by all.

The appearance in the *Ring* of the celebrated hammer of Teutondom is brief, and even briefer are the moments of its actual usage. Despite such brevity, the presence of Donner's mighty hammer adds a necessary tone to this drama in which only gods and supernaturals are to be found, and the effectiveness of that presence is greatly augmented by the incorporation into its existence of at least two of the mythical features that were associated with the Mjollnir that served as its inspiration. If the contribution to the drama of Donner's hammer is more dramatic than thematic, more theatrical than substantive, the ambience that it projects throughout the drama quite effectively adds to the mythical environment that Wagner was so intent on having. The two functions that the hammer performs are truly representative of the beliefs regarding the hammer of another day, and the hammer and its uses become another example of the mythical matters that Wagner so faithfully and so skillfully wove into the fabric of his memorable tale.

V
THE TARNHELM

During the four years (1848-1852) that Wagner devoted to the composition of the poem *The Ring of the Nibelung*, he was uniquely concerned with what may be termed, in an overall sense, *physical transformation*. Such transformations, at least in the *Ring*, are those instances when a figure of the drama changes exterior form or shape, becomes invisible, or is transported immediately from one place to another. Such changes occur no less than seven times in the drama, and six of them required some form of external mythological magic. (The seventh, which will be discussed later, was accomplished by an internal form of mythological magic.) To realize these dramatic actions, Wagner's creative thought, effort, and energy were taxed more intensely than for any other physical matter in the drama. Wagner's problem was a vexing one, but ultimately, as a result of his study of the Teutonic past, combined with certain of his own ideas, he was able to devise the needed mythological manner and magic that would allow the transformations to be made.

Wagner's solution for the problem of physical transformations was the *Tarnhelm*. This was not an object that he had found in his studies of Eddic literature. It was, rather, a singular article that his mythically oriented mind had created, a singular item for which he had devised a singular name. The Tarnhelm, which was a headcover, a kind of cap which he caused to be made from the Rhinemaiden's gold, was, indeed, a matter of his own dramatic creation, yet it was really the result as well as a reflection of a blending and an adaptation of several diverse and distinct concepts and beliefs that had been prominent in the early Germanic world.

Naturally, along with the physical Tarnhelm itself, Wagner invested his creation with the dramatic magic necessary to realize the six specific transformations that were to occur in the *Ring*. Four of these changes are to be found in *Das Rheingold* and the remaining two are in *Götterdämmerung*. The first of these dramatic scenes occurs when Alberich dons the Tarnhelm, pronounces the magic words, and then immediately becomes invisible to the startled Mime and the other Nibelung dwarfs whom he wishes to control. Shortly after this change, as a way of demonstrating his new powers to Wotan and to Loge, who have journeyed down to Nibelheim, the black-dwarf uses the Tarnhelm to turn himself first into a giant serpent (*Riesenwurm*), and then into a toad. As the argument later reveals, Fafner also changes himself into a dragon, a feat that he accomplished by means of the Tarnhelm which had come into his possession in this drama. In the fourth drama of the *Ring*, the hero Siegfried uses the magic of the helm to change himself into Gunther's form in order that he can win Brünnhilde as bride for the Gibichung. (Siegfried gained possession of the Tarnhelm when he slew the dragon Fafner and took the magic cap as a memento of his adventure.) In addition to invisibility and change of form which the Tarnhelm allowed its wearer, Wagner's creation also included another magic power, one that permitted the wearer to be transported immediately to any place he wished. Siegfried used the Tarnhelm a second time to realize this special magic when he wished to return to the Gibichung Hall after he had won Brünnhilde for Gunther. As the hero states, he drew a breath while standing on Valkyrie Rock, was immediately transported to the Hall where he spoke to Hagen with the same breath. It is Hagen who is taken by the speed that Siegfried has been transported, "in a trice" as he says.

Wagner's decision to make transformation a part of his poem was guided by a belief that was prevalent in ancient Teutonic thought. Throughout the vastness of heathen Teutondom there was a belief that certain supernatural and heroic figures could accomplish a change in their forms, a belief that certain beings possessed the magic that enabled them to acquire the physical features of someone or something else. These transformations could be realized by one of two methods: Either the figure or being itself was vested with the magic or the knowledge necessary to effect the change, or the figure was capable of causing or 'working' a special object or article to make the change. Each of these beliefs gained a most respectful standing within the Teutonic community, but curiously -- each belief gained that standing almost totally to the exclusion of the other, in separate regions of the Germanic world. In the North, in what today is routinely called Scandinavia, changes of form usually came about at the wish of the individual being, that is, by means of a self-possessed authority that the being could exercise at will. In the southern regions of Teutonic geography, in that part that was mainly on the European continent and which included most of Germany, transformations were realized, in the main, through the initiation of the powers that were unique to an article that was worn by the figure involved.

Wagner had encountered ample evidence of transformation in the mythical literature of the North. In one of the poems of *The Poetic Edda* he had read of Andvari, a dwarf, who took the form of a fish and swam about in a pool of water that lay at the base of a waterfall, and in that same poem, of Otr, a son of Hreidmar, who became an otter. In another of these Eddic poems, Wagner learned about Loge who transformed himself into a mare and then became a physical enticement to the stallion of a giant who was performing some work for the gods. Still another poem concerned Loge who was involved in another change of form in order to escape the wrath of the gods because he had been the cause of the death of the beloved god Balder. This time, Loge had fled to the mountains where, during the day, he changed himself into a salmon and hid in the depths of the waterfall called Franang. Loge's faculty for change was not limited to himself. On one occasion, this wily being transformed Idun, the Goddess of the Apples of Eternal Youth, into a nut in order that he could rescue her from an abductor.

None of these changes found its way into the *Ring*, but there were two additional transformations that are found in mythic literature which attracted Wagner because they were changes that were to be a part of his version of the Siegfried story. These transformations were the one in which Fafner was transformed into a dragon and the one in which Siegfried takes on Gunther's form. This second mentioned change is of special interest, at least from a mythological perspective, for it is the only such incident in all of the ancient literature for which there is any indication as to how the beings involved came to acquire the art of change of form. This added detail is a part of the tale of Siegfried and Gunther that is found in *The Volsung Saga*, a detail that some scholars believe is taken from a lost Eddic poem. According to the story, the art of changing forms was known to Gunther's mother, Grimhild, and she *taught* this magic to the pair.

There was yet another important transformation that was to be found in Nordic literature, one whose realization came about in a manner distinct to the usual method of change as regularly accomplished in northern thought. This change of form was made, not at the wish or desire of the figure involved, but rather by means of the magic of an article of clothing. The article was the *falcon-coat* that belonged to the goddess Freia and with which the wearer could be transformed into a falcon. This bit of mythical clothing performs its magic no less than three times in the Eddic literature, once in *The Poetic Edda* and twice in *The Prose Edda*. In the former, in that same poem which tells of the recovery of Donner's hammer which had been stolen, Loge dons the cloak, changes himself into a falcon, and flies about the heavens. It is again Loge who, in the latter work, makes use of Freia's magic coat. On one occasion, he dons the cloak, is transformed into a falcon, and flies about merely for his own amusement. On the second occasion, this same Loge uses the falcon-coat to transform himself in order that he may rescue the goddess Idun, who had been changed into a nut, from her abductor.

These several changes of form are relatively few in number when compared to those made by the champion of change, Wotan, the King of the Gods. The great god of Teutondom was renowned for his travels throughout the universe, journeys that almost always were made in distinct guises that would allow him to wander about, unrecognized. As supreme god of the world, it is only natural that the people should grant him the magical authority with which he could assume any form desired, completely at his will. Yet, the method by which Wotan assumed another form was also the method characteristic of the prevailing northern concept regarding transformation. At the same time as the god assumed a form other than his own, he usually took a distinct name, the better to hide his real identity. In Iceland and Norway alone, Wotan was known by no less than 170 names, one of which reflected more than any other this god's faculty for change of form. That name was *Svipal*, which translates as "The Changing." Most of the forms that Wotan took usually determined the names under which the god was then known. Those names are usually found as versified lists in *The Poetic Edda* while in *The Prose Edda* they are not listed, but rather divulged in the numerous tales and stories. In that same work, there is an entire story that deals at length with certain of the god's transformations. This tale, in which the disguised Wotan has the name of *Bolverk*, or "The Evil Doer," recounts how the god bored a hole into a mountain, changed himself into a serpent in order to crawl through the hole, then stole the treasured Mead of Poetry, after which he changed himself into an eagle and flew back to the Land of the Gods with the mead in his beak.

The belief in the matter of change of forms, as evidenced by the numerous transformations that are to be found in Nordic literature, was equally prevalent in southern Teutondom. Such changes of form were, however, less frequent there than in the North, and -- as already has been noted -- they differed in that they were carried out in a manner distinct from that of their counterparts in Scandinavia. If in the North certain figures were endowed with a special art or magic to will a transformation, in the south that art of change was associated with an object, and that object was usually an article of clothing. Evidence to this effect, at least as regards the Siegfried legend as well as Wagner's Tarnhelm, is found in *Nibelungenlied* (*Song of the Nibelungs*), that celebrated German version of the hero's adventures and a work that served Wagner as a primary source for his *Ring* drama. There is in this work a magic cloak which, when worn (and apparently 'worked'), rendered the wearer invisible and, at the same time, gave him the strength of twelve men. This cloak was known as the *Tarnkappe*.

The word *Tarnkappe* is a compound which means literally "Cloak of Disguise," a name appropriate for this special article. The prefix *Tarn*, in early Germanic culture, meant "disguise" or "camouflage," and it remains in modern German in the noun *Tarnung*, and in the verb *tarnen*. The suffix *kappe* is a development of the Latin *cappa* (OE - *caeppe*; ME - *cappe* and

Mod. E - *cap*), and initially meant "cloak" or "cape." In more recent times, the meaning of this word has changed to that of a garment that covers the head, such as a cowl or a hood.

The Tarnkappe has a significant if somewhat less than prominent role in *Nibelungenlied*. When the cloak first appears, it is owned by Alberich, the dwarf who is the warden of the Nibelung treasure. Siegfried subdues this Alberich and the cloak then comes into his possession. Later in the story, King Gunther requests the hero's assistance in performing the three feats of strength that will defeat Queen Brünnhilde of Isenland and make her his bride. Siegfried states that he will gladly help Gunther if he is given the latter's sister, Grimhild, as bride. Gunther agrees to Siegfried's proposal. The pair then travels to Brünnhilde's land to meet the queen in the contests. As Brunnhilde and Gunther are about to begin the trials, Siegfried dons the cloak whose magic makes him invisible and endows him with great strength. In the three contests that are held, Gunther goes through the motions for all to see while the invisible Siegfried performs the three feats of strength that defeat Brünnhilde, thus making her Gunther's bride. When the conquered woman is about to leave her land to travel with Gunther, she summons warriors, kinsmen, and vassals to be with her. Fearful of what may happen, Siegfried again puts on the Tarnkappe, becomes invisible, and steals away from Isenland to journey to the land of the Nibelungs to gather an army of a thousand men. The Tarnkappe is again brought into action after all have arrived back at Gunther's castle. Siegfried hears of Gunther's turmoil with his bride and agrees to subdue her for the king. He again puts on the Tarnkappe, becomes invisible, and bolstered by the strength that it gives its wearer, he enters Brünnhilde's bridal chamber where he overcomes the reluctant queen, and then allows Gunther to make her his bride in fact. This German Tarnkappe does not appear again in the story and no further reference is made to it in *Nibelungenlied* until after Siegfried has died, at which time Alberich relates that the cloak was *lost* at the hero's death.

It was apparent to Wagner that the belief in change of form was a regular and accepted matter throughout all of ancient Teutonic society. His concern, therefore, was not so much with the idea of transformation, but rather *how* to realize those transformations that he wished to make a part of his drama's argument. His study of the Germanic past had shown him that such changes essentially were brought about by means of two very different concepts, each predominant in specific regions of Teutondom. The composer was obviously attracted to the idea of the Tarnkappe of southern tradition which, if it did not actually grant change of form, at least it allowed invisibility, a feature that he related to transformation. Wagner's inclination toward a charmed object, rather than to the special powers of an individual, was strengthened by his awareness that despite the absence of a Tarnkappe in northern thought, there was Freia's falcon-coat which Loge had used to change himself into a bird. And, he was also aware that both northern and southern beliefs had accepted the idea that certain articles could be possessed of special magic. There was, for example, Donner's hammer which, when thrown, always returned to the god's hand. Also, there was Wotan's spear which always hit its mark and always granted victory to the god. There was also the gold ring Draupnir that dropped eight new rings of equal weight each ninth night. And there was Froh's sword which fought of itself. Wagner knew full well that articles blessed with magic powers were really a part of both regional beliefs, and his keen sense of the dramatic told him that the aura naturally aroused by transformation would be enhanced even more when accomplished by means of a charmed article that held its own magic than by the power of some unseen, intangible force.

Wagner found support for his idea of realizing transformation by means of some special object in yet another item that appeared in Nordic literature. His attention to this article was more than a passing one because this magic piece was specifically associated with two principal figures that he had included in his drama, namely Fafner and Siegfried. Wagner had read, if only infrequently, in the two *Eddas* and in *The Saga of the Volsungs* of *Aegishjalmr*, literally "Helm of Terror." This *hjalmr*, this "helm," was a head-cover which, when worn, struck terror in all with whom the wearer came in contact. In the verses of *The Poetic Edda* this Helm of Terror appears when Fafner turns himself into a dragon. The reference to the helm is succinct, stating only that Fafner owned a fear-helm of which all creatures were terrified. This poetry presents no history of the helm, and neither do the verses reveal how it came into Fafner's possession. The concept of an object that struck fear in the heart of a viewer was of no particular attraction to Wagner, but the idea of a helm associated with Fafner intrigued him. That intrigue was further stimulated when later in the *Edda* the verses tell how Siegfried slays Fafner and along with the treasure that the dragon had guarded, he takes for himself the Helm of Terror. A similar version of these events is found in *The Prose Edda*, with the added detail that Fafner had gained possession of the Helm of Terror by taking it from his father when he slew him. In the version of these events that is given in the *Saga of the Volsungs*, there is yet another detail that came to Wagner's attention, a matter that without doubt stimulated his thought about the possibility of a *helm* that allowed change of form. According to this tale, after Siegfried slays Fafner, he removes the Helm of Terror from the dragon's hoard and along with the helm he takes a *bryny that was made of gold*. (*Bryny* is an ancient word that denoted "mail-coat.")

Wagner's perceptive mind intuitively assembled all the salient factors regarding transformation that he had found in the mythological and legendary literature. He knew that the concept of change, which included invisibility, was an accepted belief throughout Teutondom, and he envisioned that his thematic need for immediate transport could readily be associated with this belief. He was aware of the numerous charmed items that existed in Teutonic thought. He was familiar with the Tarnkappe that Siegfried had worn in *Nibelungenlied*, and he had read of the Helm of Terror that both Fafner and his slayer owned. Wagner was also aware of the reference in the *Saga of the Volsungs* to the 'bryny made of gold' that Siegfried had taken from what had been Fafner's treasure.

From the mass of diverse but thematically related factors, Wagner concluded that the transformations that he was to include in his drama would best be realized through the southern concept, that is, by the magic of an object. Further consideration convinced the composer that the article in question should be a headpiece that had been fashioned from the gold that was to have such a significant role in his work. As his inventive mind created this headcovering, he realized that it was representative of a blending and fusing of the several and varied beliefs and related factors that he had encountered in both northern and southern Teutonic thought, and that whatever name this article was to carry, it too should reflect this particular union of diverse concepts. Thus it was that in the determination of what name he would attach to this distinct object, he drew a prefix from the *Tarnkappe* of the southern region and a suffix from the *Aegishjalmr* of northern Teutondom, and together these terms became a word of his own making: *Tarnhelm*, "The Helm of Disguise," the name that would identify the article of transformation in *The Ring of the Nibelung*.

As Wagner went about the business of mentally creating the Tarnhelm, and of giving it the magic that it was to hold, he sensed that its use was appropriate for all of the transformations in his drama except one, that seventh change. As his plan of the story of the gods developed, he began to sense that Wotan, the King of the Gods, the Supreme God, perhaps should be exempt from the need to resort to the Tarnhelm to effect any change of form that he might be expected to realize. Wagner reasoned that this god was the *Allfather* to the Germanic peoples, and that they venerated and invoked him as such. He considered how the early people had vested such powers and forces in the Wotan figure and that to cause this god to go outside himself for such a matter as change of form would detract from his status as supreme deity. Wagner rightfully viewed Wotan as the superior being of the universe, and he believed that this superiority must include the possession of powers that were lacking in lesser beings. It was natural for him to strive to retain in his drama the god's divine status, and he concluded that one of the best possible methods for such preservation, as well as one that allowed dramatic projection of this quality, was to distinguish the god from all other figures by allowing him to have within himself powers that were not held by any other figure, including the other gods. Wagner knew that Wotan was famed for the many guises in which he appeared as he wandered about the universe, and he reasoned that if his Tarnhelm was to hold the magic of change, it would not be used by Wotan who, unlike all others, would not only possess such authority for himself, but also the power to use it at will.

Using the powers at his command, Wagner's Wotan effects two changes of form, only one of which, however, is actually a part of the dramatic action of the *Ring*. The transformation that is not witnessed in the drama is that change in which the god assumes mortal form and achieves a union with an earthly woman, a union that brought forth the Volsung twins, Siegmund and Sieglinde. This change does not occur in mythical literature and was included in the drama, by means of dialogue, as a way in which the heroic Volsungs could be thematically associated with the gods and still be viewed as mortal beings.

The second of Wotan's *Ring* transformations has ample precedent in Teutonic beliefs. The mythical literature shows that the god traveled extensively throughout the universe as conceived by the ancient Germanic peoples. Many of these movements were to oversee the world and all that was in it. Some of the god's travels were to start, to stop, or to modify some activity. Many of Wotan's journeys were to seek out new wisdom and new knowledge, an ongoing search that was characteristic of the god. It was this aspect of the god's behavior that stimulated Wagner to cause his *Ring* Wotan to wander about, to roam at large in the several worlds of the Teutonic universe. Since the myths show that the god most often traveled about in changed form, or in a guise other than that of his godhood, and because one of these guises included a blue cloak and a wide-brimmed hat that hid one eye, so too did Wagner clothe his roving god in that same blue cloak and wide-brimmed hat that covered one eye, and it was in this dress that Wagner caused his Wotan to meet with Mime, Alberich, and ultimately with his grandson, Siegfried. It was in this guise that Wagner called his god *Wanderer*, a second name for the god which, like the other features pertinent to the god's transformation, was also taken directly from the mythical literature. So extensively did the supreme god of Teutondom travel about the universe that he was known by three specific names that all translate as "Wanderer": *Gangleri*, *Vosfud*, and *Vegtam*.

It is for all of the correct reasons that the Wotan of the *Ring* has no need to turn to the magic of the Tarnhelm for his transformations, yet it remains that this charmed article, brought into existence by the drama's author, appears to be mythically authentic. The unquestioned acceptance of the Tarnhelm as an accurate adaptation from mythical thought results, in part, from the kind of magic expected from an article that existed in a world where magic of the sort was routine. Another factor that is very much a part of this acceptance, however, is the mythos that permeated the gold with which the helm was made. And Wagner rendered all of that acceptance even more dramatically secure by providing an engaging depiction of the origin of the Tarnhelm, an origin that includes its being fashioned from the gold that had been stolen from the Rhinemaidens. This is the same gold from which there emerged a ring whose magic allowed its owner to become ruler of the world, yet a ring that also was to carry a curse of death for those who possessed it. The dwarf Alberich had made the ring, and then he had forced his brother, Mime, to make the Tarnhelm. It was Alberich, however, who had caused the magic forces to become a part of the helm and it was also Alberich who was the first to know how those powers could be worked; he had gained that knowledge from the magic of the ring.

Wagner did not depict so detailed a finish to his Tarnhelm as he had given to its origin. Rather than allowing any dramatic concentration on the end of the helm, which really would be a detraction from the main events of the argument, the composer gives an added tone to the helm's sense of authenticity by allowing it 'to fade' from the drama much in the manner that the Tarnkappe left the story found in *Nibelungenlied*. In the German epic, it is a succinct remark by Alberich that signals the disappearance of the Tarnkappe, the terse observation that "...we have lost with Siegfried the magic cloak he always wore." In the *Ring*, when Siegfried is slain by Hagen (Siegfried also is slain by Hagen in *Nibelungenlied*), the Tarnhelm is fastened at the hero's waist. No reference is made to the helm, and at Siegfried's death, the magic helmet merely has no further role in the story, it no longer is either a physical or a psychological factor.

If Wagner treated the end of the Tarnhelm much in the manner of the Tarnkappe, he did, however, make an attempt to be more inclusive regarding the last moments of his helm. The Tarnhelm and the famed ring that was made from the same gold are a part of the great Nibelungen treasure from the moment of their origin. The helm as well as the ring are vital to the rescue of Freia from the giants. However, at that moment when Fafner slays his brother and removes the hoard to a cave, the physical bulk of the gold is not seen again, and the treasure is then represented by the Tarnhelm and the ring, which next come into the hands of Siegfried. When Siegfried dies, there is no further dramatic or thematic need of the magic of the Tarnhelm and the ring alone now becomes the symbol for all the gold. When Brünnhilde removes the ring from the hero's hand and returns it to its rightful guardians, so does she return, symbolically at least, all the gold, including the Tarnhelm, to its home in the Rhine. The helm thus comes full circle, ending where it began.

Wagner's Tarnhelm is indeed a valid and significant factor in the *Ring*. It is at once an article of the composer's creation and, in a larger sense, it is a concept whose roots run deep and long in mythical beliefs. If the helm and its magic are specific only to Wagner's drama, they represent, nevertheless, not only the essence of several mythical articles and certain beliefs associated with such pieces, but also a fundamental aspect of Germanic thought prevalent in all Teutondomts -- transformation. However, there is something more to the helm than the apparent mythical authenticity that it projects and the veracity of mythical existence that it conveys. The Tarnhelm in Wagner's *Ring* demonstrates the composer's remarkable talent for adapting to his dramatic or thematic needs the beliefs and concepts of an ancient past without denigration of any kind, and at the same time, the ability to make those adaptations so mythically real and authoritative that they appear to have come, unaltered and unchanged, directly from that very past itself.

VI
WOTAN'S SPEAR

One of the more significant articles that is prominent in Wagner's poem of the *Ring*, yet one that is generally accorded scant consideration and little attention, is the impressive spear that is so closely associated with Wotan throughout the entirety of the drama. The great god has this spear in his hand or near him at all times during the drama and, therefore, its visibility is remarkable. Despite that visibility, however, Wotan's spear does not become involved in any of the complexities of the argument as do, for example, the coveted ring of gold or the sword Notung, both of which actually become central features in several scenes. This theatrical and dramatic passivity of Wotan's spear is decidedly deceptive. A more studied view of the role of this weapon will reveal that its attributes really account for the serious conflict that arises in the god's mind, a conflict that in turn causes him to act in such a way that he brings about his own downfall.

As with all else in his drama, Wagner found his inspiration for Wotan's spear in the beliefs of the ancient Germanic peoples. In the mythical literature, the supreme god of Teutondom possessed a spear, a formidable weapon which, like most other articles of the gods, held a certain magic all its own. Wotan's spear appears only infrequently in Eddic writings, but Wagner skillfully adapted it into his poem where it became the symbol of regal authority.

Wotan's spear is involved physically in only a few mythical episodes. The weapon is first mentioned in *The Poetic Edda* by the *volva*, the 'wise-woman' or 'prophetess,' who recalls the past and tells of the first war of the universe. She speaks of that war that Wotan and the other Aesir gods waged with those of the Vanir race, a war in which Wotan hurled the spear upon the enemy, an act that gained victory for the Aesir. The verses of the *Edda* also tell of yet another conflict in which the Allfather Wotan used this weapon and gained another victory. *The Prose Edda* details how Wotan will ride out at *ragnarök**, a brilliant gold helmet upon his head and a handsome coat-of-mail about his body. In The Final Battle* that will ensue, Wotan will use the spear to fight the monster wolf Fenrir.

In the heathen Teutonic world, Wotan's spear carried a name, *Gungnir*. The practice of bestowing names on certain inanimate objects that were part of the divine world was not uncommon in the ancient culture. This custom, however, was usually restricted to those articles that held a sacrosanct position in the heathen scheme of the universe. (Other such items that had names were Donner's hammer *Mjollnir*, Wotan's ring *Draupnir*, and *Eldhrimnir*, the kettle in Valhalla in which the flesh of a boar was cooked daily as food for the slain heroes who had been brought there.) Wotan's spear, as it is depicted in the *Ring*, fulfills the basic criteria that would permit a name to be used. However, as he had done with other articles of import that became a part of his drama, Siegfried's sword is an exception. Wagner refrained from using the name that he found in the myths and he also refused to give a name of his own to Wotan's spear. He preferred, instead, to convey the weapon's significance and its import by other means, principally by means of its visual association with the supreme god and, secondarily, by means of dialogue that made reference to it. An example of the latter is found in Wotan's words that speak of the spear as *Heerschaft Haft*, a phrase that can be translated as "The Haft of Power" or "The Haft of Lordship." A second descriptive phrase is delivered by the Second Norn who speaks of the god's spear as the *Haft der Welt* ("The Haft of the Universe").

Wagner's concern about the origin of Wotan's spear is obvious, as evidenced by no less than two references to it in the *Ring*. Yet, he spurned that origin that was found in the myths and he filled that void with one of his own design. The verses of *The Poetic Edda* had revealed to him that Gungnir had been forged by the craftsmen sons of the dwarf Ivaldi ("Mighty"), who also had made Skidbladnir, Froh's great ship, and the golden hair that had replaced the hair that Loge had cut from the head of Sif, Donner's wife. Wagner sensed that this origin of Gungnir could be of little use in his *Ring* argument since it required additional players who had no other reason for being, and that such an origin served no purpose, either dramatic or thematic. In its place, he put an origin that satisfied his persistent concern for the theatricality that he sought for his work, an origin that he felt was more in dramatic harmony with the ultimate destruction that the King of the Gods causes to befall the world. It is Wotan himself, in the guise of Wanderer, who tells that he fashioned his spear from a branch of the World Ash Tree. This origin is later confirmed by the Norns who also reveal that the god's act set in motion the deterioration that ended in the death of the great tree which -- once dead -- was destined to become a kind of pyre whose flames would consume the gods and their universe.

Wagner's disregard of the mythical name of the spear of the King of the Gods, as well as the rather spurious concern that he showed for its mythical origin, was matched by the scant attention that he gave to another of the spear's mythical features, its function. Gungnir was accepted as a weapon by the ancient Teutonic culture, and as a divine object, it naturally held some unique magic that distinguished it from other spears and which gave it a status that ranked it above all others of its kind. That magic so singular to Gungnir allowed that whenever thrown, it always hit the target at which it was aimed and it also brought death to those above whom the weapon had been hurled. Gungnir, thus, always granted victory in combat or battle, either to Wotan or to the warrior to whom the god had loaned the spear. Mythically, then, Wotan's spear was a weapon of war, a weapon that the god used only at such times as he was to do combat with an enemy. Wotan's struggles in the *Ring* are not conflicts or clashes of combat, battle, or war and Wagner felt no dramatic compulsion to endow his spear with any kind of militaristic character. And, in a word, the composer simply passed over completely the function of this spear as it was found in the myths.

Despite what has seemed to be Wagner's quantitative rejection, or perhaps denial, of things pertinent to the great spear of Teutondom, he was really acutely aware of the import that Gungnir had in early Germanic thought. He knew that it was not an article to be summarily dismissed, or for that fact, to be disregarded. Thus, as he had done with other articles or objects that were prominent in the Teutonic myths, such as Donner's hammer, the Rainbow Bridge, and the sword Notung, he incorporated the spear and its essence into his drama, making such changes or alterations in the article as would be necessary to meet his thematic needs, without disturbing in any way its true substance. He retained the association of the spear and the King of the Gods, but he felt compelled to alter radically the mythical concept with which the heathen culture had viewed it. In lieu of its essence as a formidable weapon of death, a weapon whose powers were unmatched and very much to be feared, Wagner completely recast the concept of the supreme god's spear. In the *Ring*, Gungnir would become a nameless symbol of authority, a symbol of the powers by which Wotan ruled the universe. And, Wagner was to dramatize that function more than once, and in several ways, as he made his way through the drama. An excellent example of this dramatization is found in *Das Rheingold*, at the point in the controversy that the gods have with Fafner and Fasolt when the angered Donner steps toward the giants and threatens them with his mighty hammer. Wotan interposes his spear and by means of its authority, which dominates all other forces, he prevents the God of Thunder from using his great strength and his hammer on the pair. At another point in the drama, this time in *Die Walküre*, the compassionate Valkyrie Brünnhilde has promised Siegmund victory and life in his impending fight with Hunding. As the two men engage in combat and fight in a death struggle, Wotan appears. The god is angered because his daughter has disobeyed his command that Siegmund should die by Hunding's hand. He then brusquely thrusts his spear between the pair. As Siegmund swings his sword at his foe, it strikes the spear and is broken, thus allowing Hunding to slay the weaponless Volsung. Shortly after Siegmund's death, Wotan extends the spear toward the gloating Hunding, waves his hand, and Sieglinde's husband falls dead. As if the foregoing scenes did not offer ample evidence of the authority that Wagner gave Wotan's spear, there are yet more. In the final scene of *Die Walküre*, the Allfather gently kisses away Brünnhilde's divinity and causes her to go into a sleep of banishment. Then, to protect his favorite daughter from danger, he commands Loge to surround the mountaintop with fire. As Wotan calls out to the God of Fire, he swings his spear so that it strikes a rock, and then he draws a circle with the spear to define the area in which the fire is to burn. There can be no doubt that this scene is an obvious display of the supreme authority that the spear carries. In yet another scene, one of the most climactic of the *Ring*, the spear -- always the symbol of divine rule -- assumes a role of critical dramatic importance. The scene comes in the last act of *Siegfried*, when the Volsung hero and Wotan meet face to face. Wotan attempts to block Siegfried from proceeding to the Valkyrie rock where the banished Brünnhilde sleeps. To stop the young hero, Wotan extends the spear of his authority. The naive Siegfried, fearless, impatient, and unaware of who it is that stands before him, brashly swings his sword Notung, and with one stroke shatters the great spear into two pieces. In that instant, the divine powers of the King of the Gods are erased and the greatness and grandeur of the god is ended. The spear by which he held his rule is no more; Wotan can no longer reign supreme as king of the gods. Wotan studies the broken spear, recognizing his own sovereign demise in those pieces. The dejected god, aware that the rule of the gods has terminated, slowly moves aside to let the hero pass. Despite the destruction of the spear and the release of the powers that it held, Wagner calls the spear into play on yet another occasion, this time in the scene of *Götterdämmerung* in which the Norns review all that has happened and then tell of what is yet to come. As these daughters of Erde tell about Wotan and the sorrow that has overcome him, they sing that soon the doomed Wotan will take the pieces of his broken spear and he will thrust the point into the breast of the fire-god Loge, and with that flame then set the blaze that will consume the gods and totally overwhelm the universe. Thus it is that Wotan's spear, powerless and without the forces of another day, still has a role in the final moments of the gods and the world that they created. (In the form in which the *Ring* is usually performed today, the fire that destroys the gods does not originate with the flames from Wotan's spear, as predicted by the Norns. Rather, the flames that ultimately set the Land of the Gods ablaze are those that have risen from Siegfried's pyre. This apparent contradiction can be attributed to two distinct stage directions, both of which are to be found in the directions that Wagner wrote for the *Ring* and in the argument itself. On one hand, Wagner gives his Norns the dialogue that indicates that Wotan himself will set blaze to the pieces of the World Ash that the god has caused to be cut down and placed around their home, the blaze that will destroy the gods. Then, later, in the final moments of the drama, after the fire and flood have ravaged the earth, the directions state that the people will look to the heavens and there see the forlorn gods sitting within a circle of fire. It may be assumed that the earlier words of the Norns have been fulfilled, and that Wotan set the blaze himself. On the other hand, Wagner also directs that the flames from Siegfried's pyre are to rise upwards, to reach into the heavens. He does not state specifically that these flames set the skies afire, but the manner in which these stage directions are set and the chronology of the stage action can easily infer that the heavens are set ablaze by the rising flames of Siegfried's pyre. It is the latter action that obviously creates the greater emotional theatricality and, therefore, the manner most often projected in a production of the drama. The fact that Wagner was not more precise in his directions, at least in the matter at hand, can be attributed, no doubt, to the way in which this part of the *Ring* was written. The scene in which the Norns appear and make their predictions was written *after* the composition of the three acts that comprise the body of what then was a single drama. Subsequently, Wagner then composed the three preceding dramas in the reverse order of their intended production. Following the compositional work, he then made alterations, modifications, and revisions within the entirety of his poem. Then, some time later, he radically revised the original ending, which is one of the scenes in question. This unorthodox manner of composition allowed much possibility of error. Wagner apparently attempted to make corrections as necessary, but it is obvious that he was not totally successful in that endeavor.)

These several actions of the *Ring* that involved Wotan's spear, and others of a related nature but of less thematic import than those discussed, give clear evidence of the spear as the symbol of sovereignty, as the visible and tangible article through which divine rule was granted and maintained. In the mythical world, this spear is not viewed in this manner, that is, it does not have such power. In the myths, Wotan rules because he *is* king of all the gods and he *is* the supreme head of the universe. The possession of the great spear is of no consequence. Wagner, however, took the mythical spear and presented it in such a way that is was more than a mere visible property associated with the god. Wagner made the spear a kind of guide to Wotan in his rule, a kind of code or standard which, at one and the same time, determined and also limited certain of the god's actions.

The added dimension that Wagner brought into the spear was made possible by the runes that were engraved on its shaft. The absolute union of the spear and the runes was a dramatic design of the composer rather than a concept that he had garnered from Germanic thought. The relationship of the spear and the runes, as depicted in Eddic literature, is only an indirect one, a relationship that is possible only because each, the spear and the runes, is individually associated with the King of the Gods. This relationship originates in "Hovamol" ("Ballad of the High One"), a poem in *The Poetic Edda* in which it is revealed that early in the time of the universe, long before the race of man had begun, Wotan hung for nine nights, head down, in the World Ash Tree. As the god hung in the tree, alone and wounded by his own spear, he saw the runes before him, lying on the ground. He took them up, and as the verses say, he began to thrive. By means of these runes, Wotan gained vast knowledge and wisdom which he would use in his rule of the universe. From that time on, Wotan possessed both spear and runes. It was at this point that Wagner took the relationship from the myths and enhanced it and made it prominent by causing the runes to be engraved upon the mighty spear, and then, together, to become the symbol of divine authority.

The marriage of spear and runes does not occur in the Teutonic myths, but Wagner obviously felt that such a union would lend phychological significance as well as dramatic importance to his spear. The composer saw himself supported in such a belief by two unrelated mythical realities which would allow him to make such modifications as he was to make. In the first instance, the runes of Teutondom were regularly written or engraved on wood. Wagner had caused Wotan's spear to be a wooden article, and not merely was it any wood: Wotan's spear had once been a part of the World Ash Tree, the holiest tree of Teutondom. From a mythical point of view, what better wood than this to serve as a spear for the king of the gods. In the second instance, mythical belief had designated Gungnir's point as one of those special places on which runes could be placed, and thus the runes of the *Ring* are placed upon Wotan's spear. In causing the runes to be engraved upon the spear of the *Ring*, Wagner was really utilizing yet another aspect of mythical thought.

Some poems of *The Poetic Edda* name and describe a sizeable number of the runes that were so vital and so important in early Teutonic life, but those verses do not specify precisely which of the runes were gathered and taken up by the King of the Gods as he hung from the World Ash Tree, and neither does that work indicate which runes were engraved upon Gungnir point. Wagner sensed a thematic need for such specificity, at least in the matter of the runes and the spear, as he developed the runic matters that were to figure so significantly in his drama. As he had envisioned those details of his *Ring* argument, it would be the runes that he would give to Wotan that would guide the King of the Gods, not only in the acts that he would commit but also in the thoughts that he would have. In his drama, Wotan would be the Allfather, the Supreme God, but he would be under the higher rules of the runes, and under that dominance much of the god's movement as well as the greater action of the entire drama could then be better understood. And so it was that Wagner developed his own dramatic details regarding the runes, and created the charmed powers that were to be a part of those bits of magic. And, to achieve a preciseness that he deemed necessary, he designated that those runes that would play such a role in the life of the gods of his drama would be the runes of *Truth*, and more specifically, they would be the runes of *truth in pacts and pledges*. Once Wagner had made his runes those of truth in pacts and pledges, he then applied to them the mythical belief that such runes, when 'worked' correctly, would be of great importance to Wotan, their possessor. The god would then be able to make the runes work in his behalf, to aid and assist him in reaching those ends that he desired. Yet, the great god was aware that if those runes were contradicted in any way, if he went against their magic in even the slightest manner, harm and ill could be the only result. It is, then, the initial pact that Wagner arranges between Wotan and the giants that sets the entire action of the *Ring* into motion, and then the subsequent violation of that pact by Wotan that establishes the serious dilemma of the *Ring*, a violation of the runes of truth in pacts that ultimately wreaks its harm in the form of devastation and destruction of the gods and the world that they had created.

It is apparent that Wotan's spear, as Wagner envisioned it and brought it into the *Ring*, underwent certain changes that set it apart from its mythical inspiration. Wagner accepted the mythical counterpart as a tangible, physical article that belonged to the King of the Gods. He disregarded its name and its origin, and he also rejected its primary function as developed in Germanic thought. Then, he brought the runes of Teutondom into his drama and created a relationship of the spear and those runes, a relationship that did not exist in the myths. And, then, to the runes of his *Ring*, he assigned his own meanings, and he designated what would be their powers. Now, the relationship of the spear and the runes elevated the status of the spear to a level that equaled and at times surpassed that of the King of the Gods who was destined to rule and to perish by its dictates.

There is no doubt that in the matter of Wotan's spear Wagner molded and adapted certain details and certain specifics of the respective myths of his culture to the needs of his dramatic and thematic objectives. It is quite evident that his creation offers several variances from the mythical substance of Gungnir, the weapon that is so prominent in mythical lore and literature. Yet, the spear of *The Ring of the Nibelung* unquestionably retains much of the essential import of Gungnir and uniquely preserves the aura of rank with which the early Germanic peoples regarded this divine weapon.

VII
FREIA'S GOLDEN APPLES

Woven into the numerous poems of *The Poetic Edda*, the work that served as Wagner's primary source for his *Ring* story of the Germanic gods and the hero Siegfried, are sundry references to items of food and drink. These stanzas reveal, for example, that the warriors in Valhalla ate only the cooked meat of a special boar who was 'raised' each day to provide an ongoing fare. Honey is also mentioned, as are certain nuts, mead, and wine, the drink that served as both food and drink for the supreme god Wotan. However, there is one edible that receives more attention in this Eddic poetry than all others, such attention that it assumes a prominence that is not only notable, but singular. This special food is the *apple*, the fruit whose mythological significance evolved from the unique role that it played in the mythical lives, and indeed, even the day-to-day mythical existence of the gods of ancient Teutondom. The concepts regarding this fruit, as well as the magical qualities that were associated with it, became so imbedded in early Teutonic thought and so widespread throughout the culture that there are still present in contemporary Germanic societies certain remnants of those early beliefs. Such is true despite the thousand or so years that have passed since the disappearance of Wotan and the body of religious thought with which he was associated.

Wagner's extended study of the Teutonic myths had made him keenly aware of the significance of the apple and the related concepts that were so much a part of that early life. He sensed the fruit's relative importance within the framework of heathen standards, and he felt intuitively the need to include that importance in his *Ring* argument. Wagner's dramatic acumen envisioned the fruit as an integral aspect of the thought and actions of his gods, and he believed that the cultural concepts that surrounded the apple would become a prime factor in the entanglements that he was to arrange for these deities.

The apple, really apples, that Wagner wove into his *Ring* argument become an integral element in the first drama of the *Ring, Das Rheingold*. The composer causes these apples to be known as "Golden Apples," and he places them in the guardianship of his Goddess of Youth and Love, Freia. Early in the drama, Freia is taken by the giants Fasolt and Fafner, to whom she had been promised by Wotan as reward for the brothers' labor on the castle Valhalla. The absence of the goddess signals an absence of the apples that she cultivated and which were in her charge. As the gods discuss what will be their next actions, they become aware that they have been deprived of Freia's golden apples and therefore the magic that they bring to the gods, the magic that grants them their youth, the freedom from growing old. Without these apples, the gods begin to age. They become sullen, they wane, and they grow pale. Wotan soon realizes the seriousness of the situation and the portent for the future of all the gods if the apples are not returned. In order to secure the release of the goddess, and therefore return of the apples, Wotan understands that he must undo the pledge that he had made to the giants by forcefully gaining possession of the Nibelung gold which the giants have agreed to accept as their payment. Thus it is that the loss of the golden apples, and all that they represent, serve as a determinative for Wotan's subsequent act of force that makes him possessor of the Nibelung treasure, an act that becomes the stimulus for a succession of incidents and events that ultimately result in the doom and downfall of the gods, the *ragnarök** of Teutondom.

Freia's golden apples are again a part of the *Ring*, if only indirectly, this time in *Götterdämmerung*, at the time of impending doom. In this fourth part of the drama, as the cataclysmic end of the universe approaches, it is Waltraute who secretly leaves Valhalla. Her journey is to seek out her sister Brünnhilde, who is now a mortal and who possesses the Nibelung gold represented by the ring. She asks Brünnhilde to aid the gods who have gathered in the celestial castle, there to await their destruction. Waltraute pleads with her sister to return the ring to its rightful guardians, the Rhine daughters, for in so doing, the initial theft of the gold by Alberich will have been righted and Wotan will have been cleansed of his wrongful act against the Nibelung dwarf. As part of her plea, Waltraute informs Brünnhilde of the disconsolate Wotan, of how he sits in silence, dejected and forlorn because of the tragic havoc that his acts have caused. She tells her sister that the god awaits the doom that he knows is to come, and in his despair he no longer partakes of the apples that once brought him vigor and vitality. Not even the magic of the apples, not even the charm of youth can entice the god to move in his own behalf!

The dramatic depiction of the magic of the golden apples of *The Ring of the Nibelung* is remarkably faithful to that found in the Teutonic mythological literature. Throughout the entirety of Eddic literature the apple was, above all else, the source of youth for the gods, a concept that is associated with the belief that the gods were not immortal. Unlike the divine existence of the gods of certain other religious beliefs, the life of the gods of ancient Teutondom was viewed as subject to the same natural laws that governed mortal life, and -- like man -- Teutonic gods were born, they grew and aged, and they died! It is obvious that this early culture bestowed some of the nature of mankind on its gods, yet it is imperative to note that this culture also acknowledged the divinity of its gods by according them a life-span that was greater than that of mortal life. Thus, if the existence of the gods was finite and they were destined to die, the time of their life was extended, prolonged so to speak, well beyond the limits of mankind's life. And it was in the apple and its magic of youth that the Teutonic culture found a means and a method to exceed the definite boundaries of the life of man and to allow the continuous presence of the gods.

The importance of the apples and their magic to the gods is clearly illustrated in a single tale that is found in *The Prose Edda*. In this story, the goddess of the apples is enticed to bring her magic fruit into a forest where a giant, who has taken the form of an eagle, swoops down upon her and carries her away. Deprived of their apples, the gods grow old and pallid. The gods are disturbed and upset, and they are well aware of the consequences if the treasured apples are not returned to them. In their plight, they ban together in a frantic effort to regain the source of their youth. Ultimately, the divine beings capture the giant, kill him, and retake the fruit that is so necessary to their continued existence.

Wagner understood fully the significance of the apple in the Teutonic mind. He understood the concept that was associated with this fruit and, more importantly, he understood the profound psychological implications of that concept within societal thought and beliefs. Wagner's theatrical acumen also perceived the potential for dramatic impact that this concept offered. When the composer arrived at that part of his tale of the Nibelung gold that dealt with the gods and their activities, he did not hesitate to incorporate the apple and its authority into the work, and to make it an energetic force in his story of Wotan's dilemma.

In *The Ring of the Nibelung*, it is Freia who is the guardian of the apples that prevent the gods from growing old. This goddess held no such position in the hierarchy of the Teutonic gods and, thus, it was by Wagner's design that she should be the custodian of the magic fruit of Teutondom. In the mythology of the ancient Germanic world it is Idun who was the goddess of the magic fruit. Idun was one of the lesser deities of the Teutonic world. She appears only infrequently in Eddic literature and she is called by name in only one of the poems of *The Poetic Edda*. Idun, who was the wife of Bragi -- the god of poetry - guarded the apples in a chest and dispensed them to the gods whenever they began to age.

The substitution of Freia as the goddess of the precious fruit of Teutondom apparently did not constitute a serious mythical disparity in Wagner's mind. He had included only five of the numerous gods in his argument, but he had been cautious and careful in the selection of those five. Wagner's gods -- Wotan, Fricka, Donner, Froh, and Freia -- were the most revered deities of the Teutonic culture, those most venerated above all others. Specific to each of these gods was a special quality, perhaps a special nature, that rendered each unique and singular to the early Teutonic mind. In addition to that special quality, each maintained a divine power of some kind and of some consequence, a force that held control of a fundamental aspect of the world or its inhabitants. Together, these five gods constituted the dominant group of deities of Teutondom, the most prominent and the most influential deities of the entire pantheon that ruled heathen Germanic religious thought. This sense of collective divine supremacy was central to Wagner's theme and to his story line. And, in an attempt to enhance even more this divine supremacy, Wagner gave his deities a familial relationship of his own making, one not found in Teutonic mythical beliefs.

Freia was one of the principal gods of Teutondom. She was, after Fricka, the most revered of the Germanic goddesses. However, unlike Fricka, Freia was venerated and she had a cult, that is, her name was invoked. Freia was a joyful, gladsome goddess who inspired love and feelings of happiness. Freia was also the most beautiful of the goddesses, and it was only natural, given the several related qualities of this goddess, that she was called upon by lovers who sought her divine favors in matters of the heart.

Wagner had come well-prepared when, in his drama, it became a matter of this respected goddess. He recognized Freia's place in mythical beliefs and, if there had been no other reason at all, that status alone merited that she be counted among the divine beings that he must bring into his story of the gods. However, it was not Freia's divine status alone that accounted for her presence among the deities of the *Ring*, but rather that factor as well as a mythological element of some significance. In his drama, Wagner causes Valhalla to be constructed by the giants Fasolt and Fafner. The work of the giants is carried out under the terms of a pact that Wotan had made with the brothers, a pact that rewards the giants with the goddess Freia as payment for their labors. This aspect of the argument of the *Ring* is an adaptation that Wagner made of a similar tale in Eddic literature. The story, which is found in its entirety in *The Prose Edda*, recounts how the gods, after they had constructed Valhalla, made a pact with a giant for him to build a stronghold in the Land of the Gods. The terms of the pact stated that if the giant completed the work within a specific amount of time, he would be rewarded with the goddess Freia, the sun, and the moon as payment for his labors. The giant, with the aid of his horse, worked diligently on the stronghold and a short time before the deadline the gods realized that the project would be completed by the date agreed upon and the giant would meet the terms of the pact. The gods were very concerned about the possible loss of their goddess Freia. They met in council and quickly arranged for Loge to help them. The crafty Loge was able to entice the giant's horse away from the work, thereby causing the giant to fail to meet the terms of the agreement and to lose the promised payment. Thus, Freia was saved from the giant. The similarity between the Eddic tale and Wagner's incident is quite evident and, despite the alterations that Wagner made in its adaptation, Freia remains as the centerpiece around which the action revolves. In addition to her divine status, the myths now had given Wagner a second reason for including her in his drama.

Wagner's union of Freia and the golden apples was to prove entirely compatible to his story. He had sensed that such an association would lend dramatic strength to his story, and he felt that the intrigue that was to be developed as the gods attempted to renege on their pact with the giants would be enhanced if the magic apples were to become a part of the payment that Fasolt and Fafner were to receive for their labor. In addition, that arrangement allowed him a means whereby the gods could be deprived of the apples and their magic, and if the gods were thus threatened by the loss of their youth, they had additional incentive to satisfy whatever requests the giants would make for a substitute reward.

Wagner's rearrangement of the heathen beliefs regarding the apples and their guardian to satisfy his own dramatic needs has been the subject of some criticism by puristic mythologists. Yet, if the matter had ever presented itself, Wagner could have pointed to at least one mythical incident that did associate Freia with the apple. The matter is recorded in the second chapter of *The Volsung Saga*, a work that Wagner acknowledged as second only to *The Poetic Edda* as a primary source for his story. In that tale, Rerir, a powerful king and grandson of Wotan, and his wife are childless. Freia appears and gives the king an apple which the king then gives to his wife. The queen eats the apple, and later bears a son. The son is Volsung who will become the father of Siegmund and grandfather of Siegfried. This brief but singular relationship of Freia and an apple apparently was a thematic attraction to Wagner, and more so probably because of its explanation of the mythical genealogy of Siegfried. It is true that the apple of this tale grants fertility and fruitfulness rather than the youthfulness that Idun's apples granted, but such a concept is not entirely unrelated to that of Idun's fruit. And so it was that Wagner had mythical substantiation for the presence in his drama of both Freia and the magic apples of Idun, and with the Volsung tale that was part of the saga, he also had mythical justification, if only slight, for the association of the goddess and the fruit. Indeed, Wagner's Freia was the Goddess of the Golden Apples!

Freia's apples in the *Ring* drama are *golden* apples! This feature of identification was original with Wagner, and was a matter that in all probability evolved out of the prominence of the gold in his story. If Wagner sensed that *golden* apples would lend a special, if subtle, dramatic flavoring to his tale, he was also assured of the authenticity of that depiction because of a single phrase that he had encountered in the Eddic verses. In a poem of *The Poetic Edda* titled "The Ballad of Skirnir," Wagner had read the tale about Froh and his efforts to woo the beautiful Gerd through his servant Skirnir. One of the gifts that the servant presents to the maiden on Froh's behalf is eleven apples which, according to Skirnir, are "all of gold." Wagner's association of apples with gold, or at least the color gold, is a matter of little consequence to any study of the tale of the gods or to the overriding forces that are at work in the story. Yet, his union of the apples and gold or "golden" is, in its own way, another of the innumerable examples that reflects the careful attention that Wagner gave to the mythical ambience of the Teutonic culture, coupled with his desire to incorporate into his poem as much of that ambience as possible.

Wagner brought the magic apples of Teutondom into his story, yet it is obvious that he was little concerned with the thematic details of the myths in which they were found. It was not that there was any lack of interest. He had his own story to tell, and the plots and arguments of the several mythical tales in which the apples were found naturally were of secondary importance to him. It should be noted, however, that as he transferred this fruit into his poem, as he wove it into the fabric of his drama, he was careful not to undue or to modify the fundamental concepts that early Teutonic beliefs had attached to it. It is true that he gave the apples their own 'golden' color, and it is also true that he placed them in the guardianship of a goddess of his own choice, and, further, that when he made this goddess the reward that the giants were to receive for their labors on Valhalla, he automatically included the apples that this goddess controlled. But, in developing his argument in that manner, Wagner was really temporarily removing this magic fruit from the province of the gods and thereby creating a powerful driving force that would compel those very gods to seek to retrieve them, to bring them back into the divine fold.

Wagner's considerations and arrangements of matters that included the magic apples of Teutondom were distinct and unique to his drama. He made certain changes, but there is no doubt that he left intact that which was fundamental and basic in the apples of the gods. Whatever changes that he made were those of a secondary nature. There are those scholars, however, who would argue that Wagner modified heathen Germanic belief to his own thematic and dramatic gain, and in so doing, wrought mythological havoc on a body of thought that represented a vibrant culture of another era. Such argument is fundamentally weakened, not so much by a defense of Wagner's actions, but rather by a careful look at the mythology itself. In a broad manner, the Teutonic myths contain a body of thought that frequently presents blatant contradictions. That thought often develops questions that go unanswered. That thought often offers a confusing, disjointed, and unclear story of the universe. No one has ever denied that Wagner, at times, adjusted beliefs to match his dramatic ends. Yet, Wagner was not unlike the culture of early Teutondom which often fashioned its thought and beliefs to accommodate the transcendent questions that it had raised. In the end, and over all objections that have arisen regarding certain of Wagner's thematic moves, he preserved and kept intact the essence of early Germanic thought, and the magic apples of his *Ring* are unquestionably the magic apples of the ancient Teutonic world.

VIII

VALHALLA

In the beginning of time, the revered gods of the ancient Teutonic peoples went about the business of creating the universe and all that was in that universe. As they created, they attempted to put all things in order, as they deemed that order to be. The activities of the gods were many and varied. One of their numerous tasks was that of enrichment of their own divine land, which was called Asgard, with their own personal dwellings, great temples, and majestic halls. So goes the tale of creation as gathered from the poetry of *The Poetic Edda*.

Among the many edifices that rose in the Land of the Gods and which bespoke that land's grandeur, there was one structure that was to become the favorite of all the gods. This building that the gods had built and to which they all were attracted was to become one of the most perdurable and cherished facets of early heathen belief. This sacred building was Valhalla, the battle-hall of Wotan, King of the Gods, and the treasured abode of the carefully selected slain heroes of the world who had been brought to the hall and there 'raised' by the divine magic of the gods.

The belief in the existence of Valhalla had developed early among the early Germanic peoples. And, the recognition of this belief, or at least recognition of the term *Valhalla*, has endured through the ages and is what may be called a popular term in numerous contemporary societies. Curiously, however, despite the early emergence of the word and the beliefs of the people that were associated with that word, the concepts of and about Valhalla did not reach their apogee of cultural religious acceptance until relatively late in Teutonic history. It was in Scandinavia, during the Age of the Vikings (800-1100 A.D.), that Valhalla was launched into a prominence of the first order, a prominence that has made it an enduring factor in much of western culture.

From the earliest of times, there existed in Teutonic thought the belief that there were two places to which humans who had died were consigned. One of these places was the land known as Hel, which was presided over by the goddess Hel, also known as Hella. The other land for the dead was the great hall Valhalla, with Wotan as its lord. Hel was a dark, subterranean land that was inhabited by dead women and children, and by those men who had died ignobly of old age, disease, accident, or in a battle in which they gave no display of heroism. Valhalla, on the other hand, was a glorious place, a mighty edifice that was reserved for the noblest and bravest of warriors, the champions (*einherjar*) who had been slain in combat. As the cult of Wotan spread throughout Teutondom and as this god's role as Lord of Warriors intensified, Valhalla gained esteem and approval in an equal manner. At the same time, there was a growing belief in Wotan as a *sky god*, that is, a deity who ruled from the heavens, one who inhabited those heavens and had his dwelling there. It was only natural, then, that Valhalla should also be viewed as a structure that was located high in the heavens, a celestial abode from which the god could look all about the universe.

The concept of a *sky god* and a celestial dwelling in which that god presided received added emphasis and acceptance during the dynamic period of exploration and conquest by the Viking hoards. That culture was to view combat and war as integral to its way of life, and Wotan was to become for the Vikings the great God of War. This was a war-dominated culture that looked upon the warrior as the true hero, a society that designated its champions by the manner in which they fought the enemy. This society of the Vikings was a culture in which a valiant death on the field of battle became an ardent aspiration of its fighters, for it was only by such a death that entry into the great hall might be gained, and with that entry acceptance as an adopted son of Wotan and a member of the god's army. It was in this society that Valhalla became distinctly defined as the abode of heroes, the ultimate dwelling for select warriors, the abode reserved for only the true champions. It was in this society that Valhalla became the most sacrosanct of places.

The name of Teutondom's most renown structure offers an interesting linguistic and semantic development. The word *Valhalla* (*Walhall* in modern German) is derived from the Old Norse *Valholl*, which in turn was a compound that had been formed of the two words *valr* and *holl*. The latter term -- *holl* - presents no serious problem of understanding to native speakers of English. The word meant "great hall" or "royal hall" and became *Halla* in Old High German and *Halle* in modern German. (The development in English was: OE - *heall*; ME - *halle*; Mod. E - *hall*, a term that acquired a meaning that was slightly at variance with that of the parent word.) The term *valr* became *wal* in modern German. (The development of this word in other Germanic tongues was: OE - *wael*; OS, OHG, and MHG - *wal*; with the variant *wuol* in OHG.)

The meaning of the prefix of the word *Valhalla* can be somewhat confusing. The Old Norse term *valr*, which is the historical prefix, denoted the carnage of battle, that is, the bodies of those slain in battle. Since *Valhalla* (*Walhall*) was the genitive plural of the nominative *Valholl*, the word, translated literally, was "Hall of those slain in battle." or in more reduced terms, "Hall of the Slain." However, there was another Old Norse word that was similar in form and sound with *valr* and which almost naturally formed a kind of linguistic companion to the original. This second term was *val*, which meant "choice" or "select." This word developed in Old German as *wol*, and remains in modern German as a poetic spelling for *Wahl* (*wahlen* - "to choose," "to select"). If the prefix word of the name of the great fortress is thought to be this word, *val*, then *Valhalla* can be translated as "Hall of the Chosen." Such an interpretation is appropriate because those who dwelled in the hall indeed had been selected or chosen for that honor. Frequently, however, modern usage blends the meanings of *valr* and *val*, and the word *Valhalla* then is translated as "Hall of the Chosen Slain."

The Poetic Edda as well as *The Prose Edda* contain numerous references, of various kinds, to this most significant structure of Teutondom. Most of the depictions are brief and succinct, but collectively they present a vivid picture of the great fortress. According to these myths, Valhalla stood in the center of Asgard, specifically in Gladsheim ("Place of Joy"), which was the land in which the King of the Gods had his dwelling. Valhalla was an imposing temple, a regal edifice with its own individual purpose, a structure that was destined to survive the catastrophe of the predicted ultimate destruction of the universe, or *ragnarök** as it was called in the original language. The entry to this Hall of the Slain was through Valgrind ("Gate of the Slain"), the outer gate that closed so rapidly that it entrapped anyone who attempted to pass without the rightful permission.

Valhalla was a large, imposing structure. The building had 540 doors, and through each 800 heroes could march abreast. (*The Prose Edda* states that these numbers were 640 and 960, respectively.) The mighty hall was roofed with shields, its rafters were spears, and above its western door the figure of an eagle and a wolf had been carved.

A noble tree grew near Valhalla. This tree was named *Ljeradr*, a term that numerous scholars have presumed to be another name for Yggdrasil, the World Ash Tree which housed the nine worlds* of the Teutonic universe. (This presumption is quite prevalent despite the fact that Ljeradr was not an *ash* tree.) Two animals chewed on the leaves of Ljeradr. One was the she-goat Heidrun that stood on Valhalla's roof as she munched the leaves. It was from Heidrun's teats that there came a never-ending flow of clear mead which served as the drink of the *einherjar*. The second animal that feasted on the tree's leaves was the hart Eikdyrnir ("The Oak-Thorned"). This was the animal from whose horns there flowed a stream that ran down into Hvergelmir ("Roaring Cauldron"), a spring that lay beneath the third root of the World Ash Tree and out of which rose all the rivers of the universe. (*The Poetic Edda* cites the names of forty rivers that originated in this spring, one of which is the river Rin, or Rhine.) *The Prose Edda*, at the first mention of the spring, names only eleven rivers that emerge. Later, however, twenty-five others are named although that of the Rhine is not among the combined lists.)

The Eddic literature presents additional details regarding Valhalla, specifics that continue to fascinate the people of several modern-day cultures. For example, Wotan's war-hall was surrounded by a river which was called Thund ("Roaring"), a river that roared quite loudly and flowed so fast that the dead of Hel could not cross it to invade the Land of the Gods. (The "wise-woman," that is, the *volva*, had predicted as part of her prophesy to Wotan that at *ragnarök** the gods would be attacked by an enemy army of the dead of Hel which would come from the north on a ship captained by Loge, and that this army would then gain entrance into the divine land.) There was also Vigrid ("Field of Battle"), the great plain that stretched far out in front of Valhalla. This vast field measured 1000 leagues on each of its four sides and had been designated as the site on which The Final Battle would take place. It would be on Vigrid that Wotan would lead his army of raised heroes against the giants and the other enemies of the gods in the last battle before the end of the universe. (An ancient Germanic custom allowed enemies to agree upon the site where they would wage their war against each other.)

The myths offer one additional detail regarding the exterior of Valhalla. To the west of the great hall there rose a giant oak tree on which mistletoe grew. This is the same mistletoe that figured so prominently in the death of the most beloved of the gods, Balder, at the hands of his brother Hod. Balder was later raised and these two gods, both sons of Wotan and Fricka, were destined to survive the destruction of *ragnarök**, as was also Valhalla, and the two were to become the occupants of the majestic hall in the new world.

The Eddic literature also depicts the interior of the stately hall in some detail. Breastplates rested upon the benches that lined the large central room of Valhalla. This brief descriptive phrase reflects what was in Germanic society the custom of placing valuables on chairs as a regular part of the preparation of a feast or celebration of welcome. In the war-conscious Germanic culture, these breastplates were considered among the most valuable of items. In this central room there was also a large kettle whose name was Eldhrimnir ("Sooty with Fire"). It was in this kettle that the chef for the gods, Andhrimnir ("Sooty-Faced"), each day prepared the boar Saehrimnir ("The Blackened") as food for the heroes who now resided in Valhalla. The flesh of this famed boar was considered to be the best of all foods and, thus, the animal was raised each evening in order that he could become the heroes' meal on the succeeding day. Wotan was always in attendance when the warriors of Valhalla dined. The god was accompanied by his two wolves, Freki ("The Greedy") and Geri ("The Ravenous"), to which he gave the food that was placed before him by the Valkyries ("Choosers of the Slain"). The King of the Gods, the Valfader ("Father of the Slain"), never ate, but rather consumed only wine, which was for him both food and drink. Drinking time in Valhalla was daily, at twilight, at which time Wotan would order that swords be brought into Valhalla, and the reflections given off by these weapons as they gleamed in the light of the fires would then light the large hall.

The *einherjar* who inhabited Valhalla enjoyed an idyllic life, at least according to the beliefs of the early Teutonic people. These individuals had been personally selected by Wotan to occupy the hall, and the god increased their number daily. The King of the Gods was keenly aware of the *volva's* prophesy of an invasion of the Land of the Gods at the time of the destruction of the universe, and as a means of defense against these enemies, Wotan was intent on creating an army that would fight these foes in The Final Battle*. Wotan was careful to choose only the most stalwart of champions, warriors who had fought bravely and who had been slain while fighting in combat. Once selected by Wotan, these heroes were transported from the field of battle to Valhalla by the Valkyries, those supernatural beings who were also the *wish-maidens* ("Wunschmädchen") to the warriors in their celestial existence. Once in Valhalla, the heroes were 'raised,' and then they were made soldiers in Wotan's army. Their activities in Valhalla included eating, drinking, gaming, and being entertained by the Valkyries. Most of their time, however, was spent in military preparation and training in anticipation of that day when they would be called upon to fight for and defend the gods. Each day these slain heroes would engage in hand-to-hand combats to improve their warriors' skills. At the end of the day those who had been wounded were healed, and those who had been slain were 'raised' in order that all could repeat the action the next day. From this depiction of those who inhabited Valhalla and their after-life existence, it is evident that the early Germanic culture considered the readiness of an army, even that of the supreme god, to be one of the imperatives of survival.

Wagner was ever cognizant of the rather elaborate depiction of Valhalla that was to be found in the Eddic literature. The composer realized that these many details regarding Teutondom's war-hall, as well as those pertinent to the inhabitants of this most sacred of buildings, had only indirect concern in the development of his *Ring* argument. However, because this temple of heroes was to play a vital role in his drama, and because he sensed that he must give more than passing attention to the qualities of those who dwelled in his Hall of the Chosen, he knew that he must somehow be quite careful, indeed cautious, to preserve the conceptual essence that the Teutonic culture had developed for this great structure.

The Valhalla of Wagner's poem is essentially the hall that is depicted in the Germanic myths. By means of dialogue and through the stage directions that he put into his poem, Wagner accurately conveyed the Germanic concept of Valhalla as a radiant, sacrosanct temple, a temple that functioned much as did its mythical counterpart. Indeed, Wagner's Valhalla is the majestic structure, the celestial fortress that mirrors the infinite power associated with Wotan. The *Ring's* Valhalla is the great hall that the giants have built so well (Loge has inspected and declared the work to be well done), the noble final dwelling place of fallen heroes.

As Wagner developed his *Ring*, he found it necessary to weave into his presentation two separate aspects about the structure that the Eddic literature had suggested to him but which in ancient thought had no association whatsoever with the celestial castle. The first of these features was the matter of Valhalla as the *home of the gods*. In his drama, Wagner depicts Valhalla as the primary dwelling place of the gods, not once but twice. It is in *Das Rheingold*, that part of the drama in which Valhalla is prominently featured, that the gods first view their shining castle and later they majestically climb the Rainbow Bridge to enter their new home for the first time. Later, in *Götterdämmerung*, reference is made to Wotan and the other gods who are sitting in Valhalla awaiting the flames that will destroy the fortress and signal the end of the gods.

In the heathen Teutonic mind Valhalla was not a dwelling for any of the gods. This regal structure was rather the exclusive abode of the slain warriors who had been chosen to dwell there and who had been brought from earth by the Valkyries. It is mythical fact that Wotan frequented Valhalla, usually daily, and that certain of the other gods, especially Freia, also visited the hall from time to time. But, none of the deities made it a personal dwelling, and, in matter of fact, the myths go into details about the actual homes that were possessed by the various gods. Freia, for example, had a large and beautiful home that was named Sessrumnir ("Rich in Seats"), which stood in Folkvangar ("Field of the Folk"), and Fricka's magnificent dwelling was located in Fensalir ("The Sea Halls"). Donner resided in the largest of all the dwellings of the gods, a home that was called Bilskirnir ("Strong"). And Heimdall, whose charge as guardian of the Rainbow Bridge Wagner transferred to Froh, had his home, Himinbjorg ("Hill of Heaven") at the end of the rainbow. Wagner's idea of Valhalla as a home of the gods apparently was sparked by the Eddic depiction of Wotan's home, and specifically of certain features of that home that he later brought into his drama. This separate and unrelated mansion that was located in the Land of the Gods was named Valaskjolf ("Shelf of the Slain"). It was a structure that had been built by the gods who had thatched it with gleaming silver. It was in this dwelling that Wotan had his primary seat which was called Hlidskjolf ("Gate Shelf") and which was the place that he sat in order to look down upon the world to observe what was taking place in the universe and to understand all that he saw. It was also in this hallowed place that two ravens, Hugin ("Thought") and Munin ("Memory") sat upon Wotan's shoulders and each morning awaited the god's command to fly out into the world to gather the news for their divine master.

The second matter regarding the *Ring* Valhalla that Wagner adapted from elsewhere in the Eddic literature was that process by which the great hall was constructed. In the ancient Germanic thought, Valhalla had been built by the gods, who had constructed it at the time that they had established Asgard, their own world, along with Midgard ("Middle Enclosure"), which was to be the world of mortals. In his drama, Wagner causes Valhalla to be built by two brothers, Fasolt and Fafner, the giants who worked to Wotan's designs and who made a pact with the god that they would receive the goddess Freia as payment for their labor. This particular arrangement, which is fundamental to the development of the *Ring* tale of the gods and the gold of the Rhine, is original with the composer. However, if Wagner's version of the construction of Valhalla was his own, and not a facet of mythical thought, it was to a similar situation in the myths that he had turned for his inspiration.

Wagner found his ideas regarding the origin of Valhalla in certain mythic beliefs that had circulated extensively in the early Teutonic culture and which were brought together by Snorri Sturluson who then recorded them as a tale in his work *The Prose Edda*. According to this story, at some time after the gods had established the land of the mortals and had built Valhalla in their own divine land, a great war was waged between Teutondom's two races of gods, Wotan's Aesir ("Ases") gods and the Vanir ("Wanes"). This war was exceptionally destructive and Asgard suffered extensive damage. The Aesir wished to have their world made strong and beautiful again and to achieve this end they entered into a contract with a giant. According to the terms of this agreement, the giant was to perform the work of restoration and then the gods would give him the sun, the moon, and the goddess Freia as payment for his work. The gods, however, wanted to protect themselves as much as possible, so they inserted a clause in the agreement that specified that the work was to be finished within a specific period of time. The giant said that he would accept their terms if he were allowed to have his stallion, Svadilfari, help him with the work. The gods felt that the giant's request was a modest one, and they then agreed to the arrangement. With both sides in accord, the giant began his laborious work. The giant was a master-builder, and with his horse available to drag the large stones to the building site, the work went well. The gods watched carefully as the construction continued. They were pleased with the labors of the giant and that the construction was progressing as planned. As time passed, however, the gods became aware that the work was being accomplished faster than they had imagined. The gods watched the giant as he worked, and in due time they became fearful that he would finish the work before the deadline, in which case the giant would have earned his payment which the gods did not wish to make. When it became evident that the giant would in fact finish his work before the deadline and thus meet the terms of the agreement, the gods hurriedly met in council and decided that Loge must come to their aid. In the past this wily demigod had given much bad counsel to the gods and therefore they believed him to be responsible for this present agreement with the giant. The deities then threatened Loge with his life if he did not help them in their dilemma. Loge was aware that the giant used his horse to drag the huge boulders that were needed for the work, and he reasoned that if the giant did not have the services of the stallion, he would be unable to finish the work. This cunning spirit then turned himself into a mare and slowly approached Svadilfari. When the stallion became enticed by the mare, the latter ran into the forest and the giant's horse followed in close pursuit. (As a result of this union, Loge later gave birth to Sleipnir, the mightiest horse of Teutondom, which became the property of Wotan and which, according to some myths, fathered Siegfried's horse, Grane.) Once he was deprived of his means of transporting the massive rocks, the giant was unable to complete his task before the deadline, and thus he was forced to relinquish what was to have been his reward. The giant was furious that the gods had violated the agreement. He rose against them, but Donner stepped forward and killed him with Mjollnir, his famed hammer. The gods had broken an oath, an action which, by early Germanic standards, was viewed as one of the two most serious of crimes. (The second was murder.) Because of this violation, the race of giants developed a profound and undying hatred for the race of the gods. This enmity was so deep and so lasting that it would be the giants who would later invade the Land of the Gods and confront the deities in combat in The Final Battle.

The warriors that Wagner chose to dwell in his mighty Valhalla, like those of the ancient myths, were only those warriors who possessed the traits and qualities of great heroes. Two such noble warriors are named in the *Ring* where, as in Teutonic myths, they are transported to Valhalla by Valkyries. Wagner's champions are Sintolt the Hegeling and Wittig the Irming. A third warrior, Siegmund the Volsung, who was conceived by Wotan in order that he could undo the god's wrongdoing, is decreed to die by his divine father and after his death in combat is then taken to Valhalla by Brünnhilde. Although the story that Wagner wove into his *Ring* has little thematic or dramatic need for any elaboration of the nature and character of those who inhabit Valhalla, he was, nevertheless, concerned that this matter be depicted accurately and properly. So it is that the composer aptly enhances the hero-qualities of those who dwell in the Germanic celestial paradise, not so much by causing numerous other heroes to be inducted into the hall, but rather by the opposite route, that is, by adjudging a warrior less than worthy of the honor of joining the champions of the army of the gods. It was on Hunding that Wotan casts the judgment that renders him less than brave and valiant, and therefore unsuited for an afterlife in Valhalla.

Although it is perhaps of secondary importance, Wagner adhered to the Teutonic concept that Valhalla was a haven reserved for males. He skillfully inserted this aspect of Teutonic belief into his drama, in *Die Walküre*, shortly before Siegmund is to meet his death at the hands of Hunding. In this scene, Wagner causes Brünnhilde to inform Siegmund that Sieglinde cannot gain entry to the heavenly abode. Wagner's dramatic reason for disallowing such an entry to the mother-to-be of Siegfried is quite logical in the total understanding of Germanic thought, yet it is nevertheless one of his own design, one that is never considered in mythical literature. According to Brünnhilde, Sieglinde cannot accompany Siegmund to the hall of heroes because *she must breathe the air of earth*.

It is obvious that Wagner's inclusion of Valhalla in his story of the gods is a dramatic acknowledgment of his recognition of the hall as one of the significant facets of heathen Germanic thought and belief. It should be noted also that he retained, unaltered, the primary purpose of Teutondom's most renowned hall, the purpose that loomed so high in the Viking culture of a long-gone era. And, it should also be noted that Wagner carefully guarded, indeed preserved, the sanctity, the nobility, and the majesty with which that early Germanic culture had endowed its hall for the heroic dead. It should also be borne in mind that Wagner thought it appropriate, possibly necessary, to incorporate into the Valhalla of his drama certain mythical material which was the substance of kindred but distinct beliefs. This dramatic blending of related as well as independent factors, a technique so artfully practiced by Richard Wagner, neither diminished nor detracted from the basic concept of the stately edifice. Rather, the result of this unique marriage of mythical matters, this union that was prompted by the remarkable dramaturgical insight of the composer, truly enhanced the cultural symbolism of Wotan's mighty battle-hall. In Wagner's hands, Valhalla retained all of its mythical grandeur, and if he made it the dwelling of the deities themselves, the great hall, nevertheless, was always something much more than a mere structure of the gods. Wagner's Valhalla became a tangible stimulus, a silent yet forceful cause for the supreme god to act, to preserve -- at whatever cost -- the issue of his universal authority, and in so doing to set in motion the actions that would result, ultimately, in the cataclysmic twilight of the gods.

IX
THE SWORD

History shows that the heathen Teutonic culture was strongly oriented to combat and to war. Indeed, the vibrant story of the Vikings, the Eddic writings, the innumerable legends, the many sagas, and even a quantity of songs that have come down to the present day give ample evidence of the existence of this cultural attitude that included a kind of reverence for its warriors and fighters, and even accorded them a singular and unique celestial dwelling after death in battle.

There are numerous and varied ways in which this ancient Germanic warlike cultural posture is revealed, and one of those ways is by references in that early literature that drew attention to the great weapons of Teutondom. In the earliest of times these peoples obviously favored the club as the principle weapon of combat. In later times the writings show that it was the hammer that had gained a vast following. Then came the period of the axe, followed by that of the spear which became the weapon most used by the foot soldier and the cavalry. It was then that the sword came into the societal limelight, assuming as it did on almost sacred status when the culture began to view it as the magic weapon of the gods.

Any reader of the vast quantity of pertinent literature soon becomes aware of the cultural importance of the sword, as well as the societal significance that it held in ancient Teutonic life. This single weapon became the means for physical survival, which of course was paramount to the people, but it also became something more than a mere weapon. As the sword assumed its elevated, almost divine, position in the cultural mind, it also became the principal requisite by which the warrior could achieve a noble or heroic status.

From the time of its introduction into the culture, the sword seemed to spark concepts that made it something more than simply on instrument of utilitarian purposes. Early on, the sword was looked upon as a form of wealth, even as treasure that was as much prized as were gold and precious stones. The sword ranked high as a reward to the valiant for their acts of heroism, for their deeds of strength and bravery, and, it was quite often that this weapon became more celebrated than the warrior who had swung it. This preoccupation of the ancient Teutonic culture with the sword soon made it the subject of song and verse, the protagonist of tale and story, and its history and its glory were recorded in the literature as well as in art, craft, and handiwork. As with other items that had bathed in the aura of religiosity, a kind of magic soon became associated with the sword, a certain supernatural power that made it worthy of special chants and charms, and the sword even found its way into the runes of Teutondom.

There were, however, two concepts that summarize more than any others the range and depth of recognition that the heathen Teutonic society accorded the sword. In the first instance, the sword, along with the spear, was looked upon as an *instrument of truth*. The sword became the witness, the attester if you will, to the most hallowed and sacronsanct of all Germanic acts, the giving of an oath, that inviolable pledge that was taken or sworn as the maker touched the blade with his fingers. Personal honor was a concern of the highest order among the early people of Teutondom, and such honor was regularly adjudged by faithfulness and honesty to pledges. Thus, the role that the sword played in such matters ranked that weapon as one of the most praised, one of the most esteemed and one of the most respected items in all of early Teutonic thought.

The second concept regarding the sword that speaks so eloquently to that weapon's place in the culture and society of that day is that belief that gave the sword its own personal god. No other item that was formed or forged or fashioned for routine use by the people of the time was held in such rank as to boast its own deity. It is true that numerous Teutonic gods were accepted as the presiders over major aspects of nature, over such matters as storms, rain, and sunshine. At the same time, it was believed that the gods also controlled much of the human condition, that is, such matters as fertility, health, marriage, love, and even life and death. Yet, singular and unique to the sword, a material object that was made by man and which served a definite purpose in daily life, was its god, a deity who was routinely invoked by the people, and especially by warriors and fighters about to enter combat. The sword's god was *Tyr* (ME - Tiw), a deity that had appeared quite early in Teutonic thought and who was to become the major god of Teutondom, the supreme god at a time before the Teutonic world had recognized its Wotan. This god is generally less known in the modern-day cultures than most of the other deities, but such lack of popular recognition does not lessen his importance in that ancient past. In that other time Tyr was not only the principal god, but he was that supreme god throughout all of Teutondom. And, like the names of the other gods, which varied according to the linguistic characteristics that developed in the several regions of Teutondom, the name Tyr also came to show the results of variations of language. *Tyr* was the name by which this god was known in the Nordic region, that is in Scandinavia. The South Germans called him *Ziu*, while in the north of that country he was called *Tiuz*. In the early days of what is now England, the Anglo-Saxons addressed this god as *Tiw*. In time, the import of Tyr, who was also accepted as the God of War, was overshadowed by the presence and powers of another god who was to become supreme throughout the Teutonic world. This latter god was, of course, Wotan. If Tyr ultimately was to fade from the thought of the Germanic peoples, he would leave, nevertheless, two indelible signs of the importance and rank that he once held in the culture. The first of these signs was the god's mark which in Old Norse was ↑, which was the sign of a rune of victory in battle, a rune that bore Tyr's name and which in time developed into the letter *T* of our modern alphabet. The second lasting sign of this early god's significance is that day of our modern week that bears his name. This day was called *Tiewsdag* ("Tiw's Day") in Old Saxon and *Tuesday* in modern English. A second early German name for the god was *Thincus* and later *Ding*, from which that language's equivalent of Tuesday, *Dienstag*, was derived.

One of the primary indications of the importance of a given object or item that is found in a society is the figurative language that is ultimately used to depict that matter. In the ancient Germanic culture the sword seems to present itself as the ideal example of such language. *The Poetic Edda*, the storehouse of Teutonic mythology, contains numerous picturesque references to the sword, references in a language that is really metaphoric in kind and quality. The Eddic verses use such expressions as *the flame of wounds* and *blood snake* as references to the sword. This weapon was also known as *biter*, and on occasion as *wound biter* and *keen biter*. Other related terms include *sword tracks* to depict the wounds that were caused by a sword, and *sword time* was synonymous with the mythical event known as The Final Battle*. The phrase "to kill with a sword" was frequently rendered as *to feed the eagles* or *to feed the ravens*, and *the swinging of swords* was the equivalent of waging war or fighting in combat. In addition to language, the Germanic culture developed what may be called *signs* that were associated with the sword. It was propitious to use a sword for combat when, for example, a warrior saw a raven, or when a warrior saw a wolf that was howling while standing beneath an ash tree, or when a warrior saw other warriors who were outside his dwelling. At the same time, there were signs that ruled against the use of the sword, such as when the warrior had stumbled or tripped as he traveled, or when it would be necessary for him to face the sun in order to fight in combat.

It was not merely with language or with frequent signs that *The Poetic Edda* exalts the sword. The verses of this celebrated work often make some kind of note of the swords that were possessed by supernatural beings of the Teutonic mythical world. There was, for example, the sword that was owned by Brimir, the giant out of whose blood, along with the legs of another giant, Blain, the gods made the dwarves at the Creation. Another sword was possessed by Volund (Velent, Weland, Wayland, Wieland), the famed smith who had used his great skill to harden the steel of his weapon. (Volund is considered to be the first swordsmith of the universe and, at times, is called *fadir morna* or "father of swords.") Another sword was owned by Vidar, a son of Wotan who was known as 'the silent god,' who used his sword to slay Fenrir, the wolf that had killed Wotan in The Final Battle*. It was in that same battle that Surt, the leader of the Fire-Giants, crossed the Rainbow Bridge and swung high the blazing sword that shone brighter than the sun. The sword that held the most magic, however, was the weapon that had been forged by the dwarves and then given to Froh. This sword was able to fight by itself when the wielder was worthy of such a feat. There is, then, the celebrated "Sword of Victory," a sword that was forged by Thjasse, a giant, who had intended to use the sword to destroy the world of the gods. However, shortly after he had finished the sword, he decided to take a nap. He was surprised in his sleep by Mimir, who put him in chains and took the sword for himself. Svipdag -- at one time a lover of Freia - seeks out the sword, confronts Donner, and with the weapon cleaves the god's famed hammer. This tale is one of the accounts that tells how Donner's hammer came to have a short handle, and also the story that claims that Svipdag then gave the Sword of Victory to Froh. (On occasion, the myths view Thjasse and Volund as one and the same being.)

There are certain swords that are part of the mythical literature and which were given specific names. The practice of attaching names to items that played a role in the supernatural world, or to swords that belonged to any of the supernatural beings, was regularly followed in early Teutonic life. Such practice, however, was generally reserved for only those articles which, for whatever reason, had gained an unusual prominence of some kind in one of the nine worlds* of the Teutonic universe. Hence, it could be expected that those swords which bore names and were part of the Teutonic mythology were weapons of great mythical significance. One such sword was the weapon that belonged to Loge, the sword that was named Laevatein ("Wounding Wand"). The crafty spirit of Teutondom had resorted to runes* to make his sword, and, as a result, the sword possessed a special magic. Laevatein was the only sword that could slay the cock who would awaken the giants in order that they could do battle at *ragnarök**, the destruction that was destined for the gods and their world. The mythology of the time held such magic so special that thieves constantly tried to steal the weapon. To protect the valuable sword, Loge hid it in a chest that he fastened with nine locks. In *The Poetic Edda*, the name of the sword that belonged to Regin, the brother of Fafner, is Redil ("Swift-Moving"). It was Regin who became the teacher and foster-father to Siegfried. In *The Prose Edda* this same sword is called by another name, Refil ("Serpent"). In the same work, Fafner the Dragon guarded a hoard of treasure which included the sword Hrotti ("Thruster"). Unfortunately, the myths give only the names of the last two mentioned swords, and no further information is available regarding the magic that each held.

It is not in Eddic writings only that special swords bore names, and ownership of such swords was not limited to supernatural beings. The custom of giving names to swords that was so evident in the mythical thought of the people had its counterparts, really its cultural source, in the world of man. This practice is depicted in numerous sagas that were to reflect the societal thought of the day, and it is evident in no less than two such works that are closely associated with the Siegfried legend, and which therefore have some bearing on Wagner and his *Ring*. It is in *Nibelungenlied*, the celebrated German epic that Wagner consulted frequently, that Iring, a Danish prince who lived in the court of King Etzel (Attila), carried a sword which was named Waske and which the anonymous author calls "an excellent sword." The poem does not elaborate on that name, but it is most probable that this weapon had withstood the rigors of numerous battles and had become, at least in the mind of the owner, a special weapon. In *Thidrekssaga*, the saga of Theodoric the Great -- or Dietrich von Bern as he is known in German -- the famed hero possessed a sword which he had named Mimung, in remembrance of his great master and teacher.

There was, however, one sword that was more renowned, more famed, and more celebrated than all others that are depicted in the Teutonic myths, sagas, and legends. This sword that has received such glory as well as praise was the weapon that was associated with the hero Siegfried. Curiously, this sword that boasts such a picturesque history and which played so important a role in the adventures of Germany's greatest hero -- including the slaying of Fafner the Dragon and the winning of Brünnhilde -- had not one, but two names. In the Nordic regions of early Teutondom this well-known sword was known by the name *Gram* ("Wrath"), while in the southern or continental Germanic regions of Europe it carried the name *Balmung* ("Destruction"). And Wagner, obviously dissatisfied with both of these historic names, gave this important sword a third name, one of his own creation. Wagner called his sword *Notung*.

It is as Gram that Siegfried's sword is known in *The Poetic Edda*, *The Prose Edda*, and in *Volsungasaga*. The word *Gram* is derived from the Old Norse substantive *gramr*, which can be rendered in English as "anger," "wrath," and "ire." The original term once existed in the early Germanic tongues but has become obsolete in contemporary languages. The story of the origin of Gram is remarkably similar in *The Poetic Edda* and *The Prose Edda*, both of which relate that the sword was forged by Regin, the smith who was Siegfried's foster father. During the forging, Gram was wound in gold and the hot fire helped to make its edge very sharp, so sharp that when it was later thrust into the waters of the Rhine, it cut in two a strand of wool that drifted against the blade. The two *Eddas* also state that Siegfried tested the sword by striking the blade on the anvil on which Regin had hammered the metal. The blow split the anvil in two.

The origin of Gram, which is so succinctly presented in the two *Eddas*, is much the same in *Volsungasaga*. The saga, like the *Eddas*, also tells that the sword was fashioned for Siegfried by Regin, but in this account the sword is reforged from the pieces of another sword. And, the story of that origin, as told in *Volsungasaga*, includes a history that is not to be found in the Eddic literature, a story that merits some detail at this time because of the influence it obviously had on Wagner and the *Ring*, especially *Die Walküre*.

Signy, the daughter of King Volsung and sister to Siegmund, is forced to marry King Siggeir. At the wedding feast, which is held in Volsung's hall, a stranger appears at the doorway, and then enters. The mysterious man seems old, and he has only one eye. He wears a cape and a slouched hat. The stranger, who is Wotan, the King of the Gods, approaches Branstock, the giant oak tree that grows in the center of Volsung's hall. He thrusts a sword to its hilt in the trunk of the tree and then informs the wedding party that this sword will be the best of weapons for him who can withdraw it. The intruder then leaves as quickly as he had entered.

Each of the guests present at the wedding feast tries to withdraw the sword from the tree. Each fails. Finally, it is Siegmund's turn, and he alone is successful in withdrawing the weapon. Siggeir, the new husband, admires the sword and wishes to purchase it, but Siegmund refuses the offer. Signy's husband becomes enraged because he cannot own the weapon. He is a vengeful person and later, when Volsung and his ten sons come to visit him, he slays the father and makes the sons his captives. The sons are bound in stocks and placed in the forest where a she-wolf eats one son a night for nine nights. Signy sneaks some honey to Siegmund which he puts on his face. On the tenth night, the she-wolf comes to Siegmund. This time, however, instead of eating him, she licks his face, at which Siegmund bites out her tongue. Siegmund then frees himself from the stocks and flees deep into the woods. His sister Signy then changes form with a witch-wife and goes to visit him, staying three nights. Some time later, their son Sinfjotli ("The Yellow Spotted") is born.

When Sinfjotli is ten winters old he goes to live with his father in the forest. For some time the pair had a series of adventures in which each donned wolf-skins and traveled about as wolves. Then, the vengeful Siggeir captures the two and orders them to be buried in a large barrow. In time, Signy is able to make her way into the mound and she smuggles in to her brother the sword that he had withdrawn from the tree. Siegmund and Sinfjotli then use the sword to dig and saw their way to freedom.

Once Siegmund and Sinfjotli have gained their freedom, they travel to the land where Siggeir lives. When they arrive, they set fire to Siggeir's hall and both he and his wife Signy perish in the flames. Siegmund and his son then return to Volsung's land where Siegmund becomes a great king. He marries Borghild and with her fathers two sons. Borghild then poisons Siegmund's first son, Sinfjotli, an act for which Siegmund banishes her from his land. Siegmund then marries Hjordis, who was also sought by Lyngi, son of King Hunding. Lyngi is so angered at his loss of Hjordis that he and his army attack Siegmund and his men. Siegmund and Lyngi face each other in combat, and as Siegmund fights valiantly and swings his sword from side to side, an old man appears. He has one eye and is wearing a cape and a slouched hat. The stranger carries a large, spear-like weapon. As Siegmund and Lyngi fight each other, the old man slowly draws near to Siegmund. As Siegmund raises high his sword and is about to bring it down on Lyngi, the old man interposes the bill of his staff. The bill touches the sword, which then breaks into two pieces. The weaponless Siegmund is then mortally wounded by Lyngi.

As Siegmund lies dying, he speaks to his wife of their unborn child that she carries. He says that this child will be a son and that he is to be called Siegfried. The dying father then adds that this son will become the most noble and the most famed of the Volsungs. Siegmund then cautions his wife to guard well the pieces of his broken sword in order that one day they may be reforged into a weapon for their son "... whose name shall abide and flourish as long as the world shall endure." Siegmund then says that the name of the sword shall be Gram.

Siegfried is born and grows into young manhood. The youth's teacher is Regin, who tells his charge many tales. One of the stories that Regin relates is the account of how his brother Fafner killed their father, took possession of his treasure of gold, thus depriving Regin of his share, and then fled and became a dragon in order to guard the hoard.

Siegfried is sympathetic to Regin and vows to avenge his foster father. The youth orders Regin to forge a sword with which he can slay the dragon. Regin sets to work immediately and forges a sword which Siegfried tests by striking it against an anvil. When the weapon hits the anvil, it breaks. Then Regin forges a second blade for the young Volsung. This sword also breaks when Siegfried tests it against an anvil. Siegfried then goes to his mother, to ask her for the pieces of his father's sword. She gives the shards of Gram to him, and with those pieces Regin forges a new Gram which, according to *Volsungasaga*, is seven spans long. (The English measurement called a 'span' equaled nine inches.) Siegfried takes Gram and travels to Lyngi's home. The youth slays him, thus avenging his father's death. Then, as in the related works, but again with varying details, Siegfried sallies forth with the sword to new and exciting adventures, including those with Fafner the Dragon and later those with Brünnhilde.

It is evident to any reader of *The Ring of the Nibelung* that the particulars regarding Gram that are found in *Volsungasaga* attracted Wagner's attention much more than the brief accounts that are found in each of the *Eddas*. The composer sensed that the saga's version of the story about Siegfried's sword, which some scholars argue is based on an Eddic poem that has been lost, contained features that not only blended and fused with his story as he was developing it, but also that these matters allowed for much of the dramatic ambience and the basic theatricality that he strove to make a part of his drama. As Wagner adapted and modified the *Volsungasaga* version of the origin of Gram and then made that adaptation a substantial part of the argument of *Die Walküre*, and to a lesser extent of *Siegfried*, he felt supported in the matter of the association of Wotan, Siegmund, and the sword because of certain separate details that he had come across in *The Poetic Edda*. Unlike the *Volsungasaga*, the *Edda* had not told of the incident in which a stranger thrusts a sword into the trunk of a tree, yet the physical description of that stranger that the saga presents is drawn from the Eddic presentations of the Supreme God, presentations in which Wotan has but one eye, and wears a cape and a slouched hat. And neither had the *Edda* depicted Siegmund as the being who had withdrawn that sword from the tree and made it his own, as was depicted in *Volsungasaga*. But, there was that one single detail in the *Edda* that in reality had served as a primary and principal basis for Wagner's tale and its relationships of god and mortal and sword. In a poem of fifty-one stanzas snd titled "Hyndluljoth" ("The Poem of Hyndla"), Freia seeks information from Hyndla, the wise-woman, and in the way of an introduction to her request the goddess speaks of some favors that the Heerfather Wotan has given the world. She says that the god gave gold to some, and to others he gave both treasure and triumph. He gave wisdom to some, and skill in words to others. To heroes he gave a manly heart, to the sailor he gave a fair wind, and to the singer his art. Included in these gifts is that which Wagner considered of prime importance in the matter of the association of the great god, the Volsung, and Gram. The goddess says simply, "And to Siegmund he gave a sword as a gift." Despite its brevity, this single line established the association that Wagner brought into his drama, and the verse assured him that his presentation did in fact have substantiation in myth, and that substantiation could be considered to be a reflection of early Germanic belief.

Wagner's dramatic treatment of the sword and related matters was obviously based on the northern or Nordic version of that aspect of the Siegfried legend. Yet, the composer had not slighted in any way the only work that was of wholly German origin and which had served him as a primary source for his composition of the text of the *Ring*. This masterpiece was the national epic of the German people, *Nibelungenlied*, which Wagner had studied quite carefully, but which offered a very different depiction of Siegfried and his sword.

In this tale Siegfried's sword is known as Balmung and its history in *Nibelungenlied* is both brief as well as episodic, developed as it is in widely scattered sections of the poem. Early in the work, it is revealed that King Nibelung held domain over a great treasure that was kept in the depths of a mountain. One day, as Siegfried the hero of Netherland watched, Nibelung's treasure was removed from the mountain. The two sons of the king, Schilbung and Nibelung, were aware that the youth was close by, and knowing of his celebrity and fame in the region, they asked him to make a division of the treasure for them. Siegfried agreed, and although he had not yet made the division, the brothers decided to reward Siegfried for the work that he was about to do. Schilbung and Nibelung then presented the hero with the sword, Balmung, which had belonged to their father. In the culture and society of that time, the gift of a sword also regularly included the first rights of an eldest son. The two brothers refused to grant Siegfried those first rights. Siegfried became quite angry, and in his anger he killed the brothers with the sword, and also slew an additional 700 of their warriors.

After this introduction of Balmung, the sword does not appear again as a principal factor in *Nibelungenlied* until the occasion of Siegfried's death. The scene is a forest into which Gunther, Siegfried, and Hagen -- and their retinues -- have gone on a hunt. After some hunting, the trio decides to have a footrace to a spring where they can drink and refresh themselves. Siegfried wins the race, but when he lies on the ground to drink from the spring, Hagen runs his spear through him, thrusting the weapon into a spot on the hero's back, the only spot on his body where he is vulnerable. After Hagen slays Siegfried, he takes up the hero's sword and hurries away. Hagen will now carry and use the sword as his own.

Sometime after Siegfried's death, Balmung is again spotlighted in *Nibelungenlied*, if only briefly. The sword, still in Hagen's possession, is not featured in any form of struggle or combat, but rather serves as a symbol of the hero whose property it once was and as an effective stimulus to intensify in Grimhild, Siegfried's widow, the grief and emotional pain that she has suffered because of her husband's death. The setting is a courtyard of the palace of Queen Grimhild. The queen, who is aware that it was Hagen who slew the hero, has greatly mourned the loss of her beloved. Hagen and a friend are seated in the courtyard. The friend informs Hagen that the queen and her entourage are approaching and suggests that the two rise as she passes, as was the courtly custom.

The arrogant Hagen refuses to stand to recognize the queen. He insists that to rise for her majesty would be interpreted by Grimhild's court of warriors as a sign of fear rather than one of respect for royalty.

As the queen nears the pair, Hagen remains seated and in a show of defiance, he places Balmung across his knees. When Grimhild sees the sword so placed, and in the possession of her husband's murderer, her sorrows are revived and she begins to weep.

The scene is important for something more than its display of Hagen's insolence and Grimhild's sorrow. It is in this scene, the only one of its kind in the entire *Nibelungenlied* that there is to be found description in any form of Balmung. The anonymous author wrote simply that Balmung was a gleaming sword, and that it was sheathed in a bright red embroidered band. The hilt that extended from this sheath was all of gold, and inlaid in the pommel of that hilt was a gemstone that shone greener that the grass. Other than these few words that adorn this segment of the tale, the epic poem of the German people does not offer any other details or any other description of the most famous weapon in all of Germanic history.

The third scene in *Nibelungenlied* in which Balmung plays a role is essentially the segment that concludes the poem. The hero Dietrich von Bern does battle with Hagen and although he is fearful of the mighty Balmung, he is victorious in combat and overcomes the arrogant vassal of the Burgundian kings. When Hagen is brought in fetters before Queen Grimhild, Dietrich pleads for this man who had fought so valiantly, asking the queen that he not be made to suffer. The queen stares intently at this man who killed her husband, this man whom she hates so intensely and on whom she has sworn to take vengeance. After a moment of silence, the queen finally declares thst she will grant Hagen his freedom if he returns to her the treasure thst Siegfried had won but which he had seized after the hero's death and which he had then sunk in the depths of the Rhine. The haughty Hagen refuses Grimhild's request. The queen laments Hagen's words, but adds that at least she will have her husband's sword, the sword that Siegfried was wearing when last she saw him. Using both hands in what was almost a simultaneous motion, Grimhild grabs the sword, draws it from its sheath, and raises it high above her head. In a final moment of revenge, the queen then brings the sword down with a mighty swing, and with the blow, she strikes off Hagen's head.

It is obvious to the reader of both the northern and the southern versions of the Siegfried story, as developed in *Volsungasaga* and *Nibelungenlied* respectively that Siegfried's sword figures less prominently and less frequently in the deeds and adventures of its hero-owner in the epic poem than in the northern saga. Although the southern poem grants a certain majesty and nobility to Siegfried's sword, and allows it to become the instrument that avenges the hero's death, its history is relatively sparse. In *Nibelungenlied* the emphasis is placed more on the characters and their actions rather than on the weapon. Unlike *Volsungasaga*, where the sword has a significance that is obvious and primary to the story, in *Nibelungenlied* it is almost as if the sword bears a secondary importance, a depiction that the weapon is there only because it is a necessary part of the culture. Wagner obviously sensed this thematic and dramatic difference in the two presentations of the sword and concluded that the specifics of the Gram of Eddic and saga literature were more compatible with the thematic needs of his *Ring* than those of the Balmung of the literature of his native land. Yet, if Wagner turned more to the Nordic element for his story line, he would not forget the courtly and chivalric overtones of his German source.

There can be no doubt that Wagner understood the fundamental significance of this famed sword of myth and legend and epic poetry. And, he was equally aware of the need to invest the sword of his Siegfried with those qualities that conveyed such an understanding. This sword was first and foremost a weapon, a mighty weapon. It was the primordial sword Gram, the Eddic sword that was forged to slay a dragon. At the same time,

Wagner viewed this sword as the Gram of *Volsungasaga* a sword that was enveloped in the mystery of the stranger who thrust it to its hilt in the trunk of a tree. It was a sword that somewhat magically was broken into two pieces by that very stranger, a sword that later was to be reforged before it became a factor in the adventures of its owners. In a third vein, Wagner realized that Siegfried's sword was also Balmung, the sword of the German *Nibelungenlied* a sword of beauty and majesty, a sword that was wielded by a valiant, fearless and noble hero. Wagner's pride in his native culture and his sense of nationalism ran deep within him as he went about developing his 'German' work of art, and it was almost natural that he give the name of Balmung to the sword that his Siegfried was to carry. However, as those close to the composer became familiar with his drama, they began to question the wisdom and the propriety of Balmung as a name for this weapon. The ambience of the *Ring* was not that of the elegant courtly atmosphere that highlighted *Nibelungenlied*; it was of a more mythical quality, that of an ancient time, and it was awash with the heathen religiosity that flowed naturally from the presence of the deities and the other supernaturals who were so much a part of his story.

If these matters caused Wagner to ponder the mythical validity of Balmung as a name for his sword, there was a thematic aspect of his *Ring* argument that decisively convinced him that *neither* the Gram of myth nor the Balmung of legend was the sword of his drama, and therefore neither name was appropriate as the name for his sword. As he adapted into his tale the *Volsungasaga* version of the origin of the sword, he had presented Siegmund as a weaponless mortal who had been challenged to combat by an angered Hunding in whose dwelling the Volsung had sought refuge. As Siegmund related the story of his troubled life, Wagner included a detail of his own dramatic creation, a detail that was not a part of the mythic or legendary history of the sword, but one that ultimately would become the basis for the name given to the sword. As part of the story, Siegmund reveals that his father had promised him a sword, a weapon that would come to him *in the hour of his greatest need*. Siegmund's time of need had arrived; he stands without a weapon and he must face Hunding in combat. Then, as Sieglinde tells him of the sword that lies buried in the tree that rises in the room, the sword that was placed there by a stranger and which no one has been able to withdraw, Siegmund is certain that this is the sword that was promised to him. Joyful in the love that he has found in Sieglinde and with the name of *Siegmund* (Figuratively - "Guardian of Victory") that she has given him, the Volsung approaches the tree. Declaring that both Sieglinde's love and the sword have been what he has lacked in life, and that both have come to him at the time of his greatest need, Siegmund triumphantly withdraws the sword and in a moment of exaltation names it *Notung*.

The term *Notung* is one of those numerous words of the *Ring* text that is of Wagner's own creation. He conceived the word as a compound, formed with the two substantives *Not* and *Ung*. The prefix *Not*, which translates literally as "need" or "want," with an associated inference of "emergency," is derived from the Old Norse *Naud* (OHG and MHG - *Not*; OS - *nod*; OE - *nied, nyd, ned*). The parent *Naud* was something more than a word that existed as a part of the ancient Germanic languages; it was a special term in that it was the name of a rune which, when 'worked' properly, prevented the wife of another from betraying a man's trust. The mark of this rune was ⌐\, and according to the mythical literature, it could be made on a drinking horn or on the back of the hand. In time, as some of the runic marks became associated with alphahets, ⌐\ developed into the letter *N*. Although Wagner was little concerned with *Naud* as a rune, there was, without doubt, the realization that the word was a prominent term in that it represented one of the most salient concepts of the ancient Germanic culture and, at the same time, had a meaning readily adaptable to his argument. (It is possible, although highly improbable, that Wagner rationalized that he was making his sword a very German sword, in the pattern of his 'German' work of art, when he gave it the name of Notung. The German epic that today is known as *Nibelungenlied* and which is considered to be a primary source to Wagner for his *Ring* drama, had as its original title *Nibelungen Not und die Klage*.)

The suffix *Ung* denoted, among other things, "child of" or "offspring," and when joined with *Not*, the compound meant "child 'born' of need." Wagner sensed that this literal meaning of the word *Notung* could also be interpreted figuratively, that Siegmund's sword was, indeed, an 'offspring born of need,' and that interpretation could easily be related to Siegmund's plight, a plight in which the sword came to him in the time of his greatest need. The sword, indeed, was very much the "child of need," a *Notung*, a name that aptly blended with the situation at hand. (It should be noted that Wagner used the suffix *Ung*, in the sense of "child of," on at least three other occasions in the *Ring*: Siegmund is a *Wälsung* Volsung, that is, a "child of Wälse"; Gunther, like his sister Gutrune, is a *Gibichung* or "child of Gibich"; Alberich, among others, is a "child of Nibel," and therefore a *Nibelung*. *Nibel* is a variation of *Nebel* - "mist," "fog.")

The name *Notung* and the significance of that name are specific to *The Ring of the Nibelung*. Although Wagner incorporated into his weapon much of the concept of the mythical Gram and, if to a lesser extent, also that of the legendary Balmung, he understood that in reality his sword was neither of the two that had come before, that his sword was distinct, that it existed as a weapon closely related to the action that he had woven into his version of the story of Wotan, Siegmund, and Siegfried. In this light, the sword was a special weapon, worthy of a special name, one that loaned itself to the uniqueness of the blade's origin and which, at the same time, conveyed an essence that epitomized the situation at hand.

There can be no doubt that Wagner looked upon the sword of his drama with special favor. As Notung makes its way through the greater part of the *Ring*, from its initial appearance in the trunk of a tree to its unobtrusive demise at the death of Siegfried, it would seem that Wagner was paying his sword a kind of personal homage. As the sword becomes integral to the deeds and actions of Siegmund, and then to those of Siegfried, it would seem that Wagner was guided by a powerful desire to interlace in his drama a certain ambience, a certain feeling that he hoped would be sensed by all. And, perhaps he had taken his dramatic cue in this regard from some verses in *The Poetic Edda*, verses in which a Valkyrie tells of some swords that are hidden on an island, among which is one that stands out from all the others. As the Valkyrie talks of this sword, her words synthesize all that Wagner was attempting to bring to his sword. The Valkyrie says:

> Fifty there are save only four;
> One there is that is best of all,
> The shield destroyer, with gold it shines,

On its hilt is fame, in the haft is courage,

In the point is fear for its owner's foes.

This Eddic stanza does not clarify the substance of its verses, that is, there is no way to ascertain to which, if any, specific sword the verses make reference. It would appear that the references, lacking a proper name, are not to the mythical sword Gram. Neither can they possibly infer the sword of the *Ring*. There is in their imagery, however, a depiction that shares an intimacy that Wagner sought to make a part of his Notung, a special sword for which he created a special name.

X
THE RING

One of the prominent features of the behavioral history of countless societies has been the use of rings to adorn parts of the human body. Such practices originated in prehistoric times, and ultimately became so accepted within many cultures that the respective languages of those cultures often developed distinct words to denote these rings. The terms that are used often differentiate rings according to the parts of the body that are involved, or according to the symbolism that the rings represent, and occasionally, to the use to which the rings are put. These vocabularies, exclusive of their adequacy for word adoption, vary greatly, dependent in large measure on the traditions of the culture that evolved in the past, and the extent to which the use of rings was and is practiced. In modern English, as an example, there are the terms *bracelet*, *necklace*, and *earring*, each a single word that denotes a "ring" that is used or worn on a specific part of the body. This same language also recognizes *wedding ring, engagement ring, arm ring,* and *nose ring* as types of rings which, if not single words, are nevertheless terms that denote rings that are worn on specific parts of the body. Most other languages can show parallel linguistic patterns and developments in their vocabularies.

There is one type of ring that, more than any other, has gained what can be termed a universal popularity. This ring is the *finger-ring*, a somewhat generic term, but nevertheless one that denotes a use of a ring that not only has acquired general cultural acceptance, but also has withstood the numerous and sometimes radical changes in thought brought on by time, and by society itself. This use of the finger-ring is to be found in wide use among the earliest of the Teutonic people, and the extent to which it was used, as depicted in the mythical literature, becomes a concrete indication that the ring as an adornment had become a very special matter, even in that ancient society. In his study of the Germanic past, Wagner became aware that the ring had played a fundamental, indeed a significant role in the culture of these peoples, and it would be he who would bring that same attitude and the intensity of that concept of the ancient culture into the drama that was to be his *Der Ring des Nibelungen*. Wagner would make the ring the dramatic centerpiece in the complex maze that became his four-part drama, his ring would become the stimulus for all major acts and actions. Indeed, to know the path of Wagner's ring in his poem, and to know why this ring is so coveted, is to know at once the story and the essence of that story.

Rings are mentioned rather frequently in Eddic literature, and the different situations in which these rings are found become representative of the several varied concepts that are attached to these cherished items of jewelry. First, and perhaps foremost, the ring in early Teutondom was regarded as 'treasure,' or 'wealth,' fashioned as they usually were of gold, and often inlaid with jewels or gems. It is, for example, Sigrlin, the daughter of a king, who displays her wealth by means of the many rings that she wears. ('Treasure' often included the concept of 'beauty,' as in the case of Sigrlin whose numerous rings set off her physical beauty.) The wealth of the warrior Helgi is predicted when a Valkyrie tells him that one day he will possess a hoard of rings, a wealth that befits his status as a hero. It is Volund, the smith, who watches over a treasure of 700 rings that he had made of gold and gems, and which he has carefully strung on a cord.

The societal standard that designated rings as wealth and treasure recognized a second concept regarding these same objects that was quite prevalent in ancient Teutonic thought. Rings were prized as gifts, both to be given and to be received. It is from the smith Volund, for example, that King Nidud's men steal a ring in order that the king can make a present of it to his daughter, a gift that later proves to be the girl's undoing. Another Eddic example is that of Helgi, the hero, who sought to win Svava, the daughter of

King Eylimi, with a gift of rings. Another example of the high regard that the people had for rings is shown in the matter of Gutrun who, after she had slain her two sons who had been fathered by her husband Atli (Attila), distributed treasure to her husband's warriors as a means to prevent their anger and their wrath at her actions. That treasure included, among other valuable objects, "rings of red gold." Among the gods, it was Bragi, the God of Poetry, who promised Loge the gift of a horse, a sword, and a ring if the shrewd demigod would refrain from revealing certain intimate details about the life of the gods. It is the supreme god Wotan who rewards the *volva*, the prophetess, with a ring, in exchange for the knowledge that she possesses, and in a similar vein, Siegfried presents Brünnhilde, a shield-maid who gives aid to kings in battle, with a ring as reward for the wisdom that she has revealed to him.

Early Teutonic culture recognized the ring as the appropriate symbol to be used during the rites and rituals of marriage. Prior to the wedding itself, a ring was acceptable as the bridal fee, the customary payment that was offered to the parents of the bride by the prospective groom. In the ceremony of marriage, the pronouncement of vows was traditionally accompanied by an exchange of rings, an action that symbolized the sanctity of those vows, much as the spear, and later the sword, guarded the sacred truth of an oath or pledge. Such practice is even recorded in Eddic poetry, in *The Poetic Edda*, in the poem that bears the title "The Song of Rig." In this poem Heimdall, the god who is Guardian of the Rainbow Bridge, and watchman for the gods, goes forth into the world of mortals as Rig. The verses then tell how Rig fathered the first person of each of the castes of early Teutonic society. The particular scene in question tells how Rig's son Karl ("Yeoman") and Snor ("Daughter-in-Law"), the couple whose children will become the farmers of the world, presented rings to each other as tangible symbols of their betrothal.

In addition to the heathen Teutonic use of rings as treasure, as gifts, and as the symbol of marriage, the culture also regarded rings as material signs of welcome. This was a practice that was followed at all levels, even by the gods. In the Eddic poetry, it is no less a figure than the supreme god Wotan who sees that the seats of Hel are bedecked with gold and the benches are bright and gleaming with rings! This scene is depicted in the poem "Balder's Dream," whose verses then tell how Wotan is puzzled at what he has seen and who then asks the prophetess why these preparations have been made. The answer is not one that the god wished to hear: The *volva* tells Wotan that the hall is prepared to give welcome to Balder, Wotan's favorite son, as he travels to the underworld in his death!

The ring had yet another use, it could convey a message. The mythical literature tells of Guthrun who wrapped the hair of a wolf around a ring and sent it to Gunnar and Hogni, who immediately understood that the ring so prepared was a warning of impending danger. In another Eddic poem Guthrun consults the magic of a ring and foresees the death of Atli, a death by fire that soon occurs.

Of the numerous rings that are mentioned in the Teutonic mythical literature, and the assorted uses to which these rings are put, there are two that are more celebrated and more prominent than any others. The first of these renowned rings bore the name *Draupnir* ("Dropper"), and it belonged to the King of the Gods, Wotan. Curiously, the name of this ring was also the name of one of the dwarves who came into existence at the time of the creation of the universe. According to *The Prose Edda*, Draupnir had been made of gold by two dwarves, Brokk and Eitri. These smiths were the brothers who also forged two other treasures that belonged to the gods: the hammer Mjollnir that was owned by Donner, and the boar with golden bristles that was given to the god Froh. Each of these three marvels of the smiths' art held a special magic, and that of Draupnir allowed it to drop each ninth night eight gold rings, each of which was the same weight as the original.

Apparently Draupnir had a special meaning for its owner, Wotan. The Eddic literature tells that the god and his wife Fricka were greatly saddened at the death of their favorite son, Balder. The supreme god was so stricken by this tragedy that he traveled to where Balder's body lay, and there, while in great sorrow, he placed Draupnir on the pyre whose flames were to consume Teutondom's favorite god. This was the same pyre that Donner had consecrated with his hammer. This tale, as told in *The Prose Edda*, relates how Balder was so desirous to return the ring to his father that he gave Draupnir to Hermod, another of Wotan's sons, who had ridden to the goddess Hel to ask her, on Wotan's behalf, that she release him. The details of this mythic story vary somewhat in *The Poetic Edda* in that the version in verse tells that the ring was consumed in the flames of Balder's pyre. This same *Edda* also contains a poem in which Draupnir served as a gift that Froh causes to be given to Gerd, a young maiden whom the god wishes to win over. (It should be noted that the myths do not reveal how Froh came into possession of this famed ring.) In yet another poem of *The Poetic Edda*, it is on Draupnir that Wotan swears an oath, an act that is of singular importance within the Teutonic scheme of things. Wotan's pledge proves to be a false one, and the entire matter initiates a series of events that leads ultimately to *ragnarök**, the destruction and downfall of the gods and the disintegration of their universe.

Draupnir was indeed one of Teutondom's most important rings, but it was not this ring that attracted most of Wagner's dramatic attention as he developed the story line that was to be his *Ring*. There was another ring that was to be found in the myths, a ring that students of the Wagner drama will acknowledge immediately as an object that became very much a part of the composer's thought as he concentrated on the argument of his drama. It was not that Wagner was drawn to this second ring because of any special or unique magic that it held, or because it was so prized by the gods. Rather, the entire matter revolved around the tale in which the ring appears, a story that obviously inspired Wagner and became primary as he worked on his version of Teutondom's mythical and legendary past. The tale of this second ring is to be found in the two *Eddas*, with only minor variations, and its relevancy to Wagner's *Ring* argument merits its retelling here in some detail.

The Allfather Wotan, the god Honir, and Loge were on a journey. At one point in their travel the trio came to a waterfall in which there were numerous fish swimming about in the water. One of the fish was really the dwarf Andvari who watched over a treasure of gold that he had brought to the waterfall. Andvari did not live in the waterfall because he desired to live there, but rather because he had been fated to this existence by a Norn. Andvari swam about in the waters of the fall, always watching over his gold. Otr, the son of Hreidmar and brother to Regin and Fafner, regularly went to the fall, and one day when he reached the water's edge he changed himself into an otter, caught a salmon, sat on the bank, and then -- with his eyes closed -- ate the fish. While Otr was eating his catch, Loge threw a stone at him. The rock hit Otr and killed him. The three travelers then removed Otr's skin, believing that such an act would bring them good luck. That night the trio sought lodging at a dwelling that happened to be the home of Hreidmar and his sons. When Hreidmar was shown the skin of his son, he and the remaining two sons seized the three. Hreidmar now demanded payment from them for his son's life. He ordered that his son's skin be filled with gold. Neither Wotan nor Honir had brought along any gold, and so they commanded Loge to secure whatever quantity of the precious metal that was necessary to meet the father's demand. To comply with the gods' order, Loge went to the waterfall where Andvari lived. Loge soon caught the unwary fish in his net. Loge threatened Andvari with his life and the dwarf was forced to turn the treasure over to him.

Andvari surrendered all of the hoard, all that is except a ring, which Loge also demanded. This ring was called *Andvaranaut* ("Andvari's Gem"). When Andvari was forced to give up his ring along with the hoard, he pronounced a curse of death on all who came into possession of the gold. (A variation of this aspect of the tale that is found in *The Prose Edda* and *Volsungasaga* is that Andvari put the curse only on the ring rather than on all the treasure.) Loge returned to his companions with the treasure from the waterfall. The three then stuffed the gold into Otr's skin and when it was filled they stood the skin on its feet. The father now demanded that more gold be placed around the skin, enough that he would not be able to see his son. The two gods and Loge did as Hreidmar had demanded, but they held back the ring. When the trio had finished its work, Hreidmar could still see one of his son's whiskers, which Wotan then proceeded to hide from view with the ring. When Hreidmar could no longer see any part of his son, he gave the trio its freedom.

After Wotan, Honir, and Loge had departed, the son Fafner then slew his father and took all the gold for himself. Fafner then fled to Gnitaheith where he changed himself into a dragon to guard over the gold. Later, the hero Siegfried slew Fafner and gained this vast hoard for himself, including the ring. Siegfried then went on to seek other adventures and in the course of his heroic life he wed Gutrune, to whom he gave Andvaranaut as a present. In time, Siegfried is slain, and Gunther and Hagen then take possession of the treasure. Siegfried's widow is then forced to wed Atli of Hun Land. When Atli invites Gunther and Hagen to visit his land, Gutrune fears treachery. To warn her brothers, she sends them a message in runes, and as a token she sends the ring Andvaranaut with a wolf's hair tied into it.

Andvaranaut is less prominent in *The Prose Edda* than in its poetic counterpart but, nevertheless, this ring does have a role in that work's version of the tale that tells of Siegfried and how he wins Brünnhilde as a bride for Gunther. There are variations in the Eddic literature regarding *when* this action occurs as well as variations in the figure of Brünnhilde and her relationship to others, but this prose tale relates that Siegfried overcame Brünnhilde and the next morning presented the ring Andvaranaut to her as a gift. The ring is not called by name in this version, but it becomes apparent that it is Andvaranaut when the gift is identified as the gold ring that Loge had taken from the dwarf Andvari.

The importance of rings in the culture, as manifested in the myths, is beyond question. The frequent references in the literature, the several uses to which rings were put, the fact that several rings have proper names, and the special regard that are shown for Draupnir and Andvaranaut are ample evidence of the significance that this form of jewelry commanded in early Teutonic thought. It should be recalled also that Draupnir belonged to no less a being than the King of the Gods, and that Andvaranaut played a role in the legend that developed around one of the Germanic culture's most durable and beloved heroic figures. Such evidence must be seriously considered.

Wagner was doubtlessly aware of the status of the ring in the heathen culture and its prominence in the mythical literature. This awareness and the knowledge that evoked it allowed the composer not only to include such an object in his drama, but also to place that object in the dramatic forefront of his argument. Wagner caused his ring to become specific in his drama, to take on a form and substance that would be unique and individual, yet at the same time to be very much a ring like those that were part of the ancient

Teutonic thought. Wagner's ring, essentially, was developed from the generic totality of the rings that he had found in the myths, and as such it was a reflection of mythical beliefs, a ring like others that were part of Eddic literature. Like those rings of old, Wagner's ring was *treasure*, forged as it was from the gold that had rested in the Rhine. Wagner's ring had been forged by the artisans of the Teutonic world, the dwarves. If Wagner's ring had been fashioned by only one dwarf, and not by two as had worked on Draupnir, the music-drama's depiction nevertheless projected the concept that it was the dwarves of the universe who were the workers of precious gold, the talented craftsmen who fashioned the marvels of the universe. Like the ring that was stolen from Volund, and like that taken from Andvari, Wagner's ring was taken by force from its owner. When the ring was taken from Andvari, the dwarf reacted by placing a curse of death upon it. When the ring was taken from Alberich, the dwarf reacts by placing a curse of death upon it. As the Eddic trio of Wotan, Honir, and Loge attempted to ransom themselves by covering the skin of the slain Otr with gold taken from a dwarf, so too do Wagner's gods seek to secure their release from a pledge by covering the goddess Freia completely with the gold that they had taken from the dwarf Alberich. In the mythical writings the ring Andvaranaut is used to hide one of Otr's whiskers in order that the father may no longer see his son. In the *Ring*, Wagner's ring becomes the item that seals the chink through which the giants could still see Freia. In the mythical literature Fafner slays his father in order to get the ring and the hoard. Wagner causes his Fafner to slay his brother. As in the myths, so too in Wagner's drama does Fafner flee with the ring and the hoard and later change himself into a dragon in order to lay guard over the treasure. Like the Regin of myth, Wagner's Mime serves Siegfried, all the while coveting the treasure and the ring. Wagner's Siegfried, like the hero of mythical literature, seeks out the dragon, slays him, secures the ring for himself, and than later presents it to Brünnhilde as a gift. There can be no doubt regarding the source that gave rise to the ring in *The Ring of the Nibelung*.

There is, however, one major attribute of the ring of Wagner's drama that the composer did not adapt from the numerous features of rings that he had found in the mythical as well as in the legendary literature. This attribute is revealed early in *The Ring of the Nibelung*, in the opening scene, when the dwarf Alberich learns from the Rhinemaidens that the one who forswears love can make a ring from their gold, *a ring that will grant its owner mastery of the universe.* As Wagner told his story of the gods, he wove into the character of certain of his figures, principally Alberich, Mime, Hagen, and Wotan, a desire to dominate, the urge to control, a greed, or perhaps it may be called a lust, for power and command over others. When Wagner invested his ring with the magic that allowed its owner lordship of the entire world, he was giving himself a dramatic means with which he could set his figures one against the other, a means by which he could involve them, in a most natural way, in schemes and devious plots to gain possession of that ring, even to thoughts of murder. This feature is one of singular and fundamental import to the entirety of the argument of the *Ring*, one which catapulted the ring to a position of absolute dramatic prominence, an attribute that made the ring stand above all other property items of the drama.

There is no ring in mythical thought or literature that was possessed of that magic that gave its owner mastery of the world. Yet, this feature that Wagner brought to his ring was not entirely his own, he had found a similar matter in a work of his native land, the German epic legend *Nibelungenlied*. More precisely, Wagner had concerned himself with an *aventiure*, or chapter, of this poem in which he had encountered a legendary source for the magic of his ring. This segment of the German epic tells of the disposition of the great Nibelung treasure after the death of its owner, Siegfried. The hero's widow, Lady Grimhild, had claimed the hoard as her inheritance and had sent 800 of her men to where the treasure lay deep within a mountain. There was so much gold and so many precious jewels that it required twelve wagons, each making three trips a day on each of four days and nights, to transport the hoard to the ships that would bring it up the Rhine. Among all of this treasure there is one item that is more perfect than all else because it holds a special magic. This object is a *wishing-rod*, and the legend states that the one who knows its nature can become "... master of every man in the whole world." Curiously, nothing more is ever revealed in *Nibelungenlied* or in any other literature about this magic rod. (The remainder of the segment that tells of the hoard reveals that Hagen later stole the treasure from Queen Grimhild and sank it in the Rhine.)

Wagner's intuitive mind grasped the theatrical possibilities of the marvel of the German wishing-rod and he did not hesitate to transfer the concept of its magic to the ring that is forged by his Alberich. It is evident that the composer sensed that this magic was entirely compatible with mythical beliefs that were associated with rings and, after all, was not the ring of his drama to be made of gold -- as was the wishing-rod -- and was not his ring to be a part of the great treasure that figures so prominently in myth and legend, as well as in his drama!

Wagner's ring represented a balanced thematic blend of concepts that are to be found in both northern Germanic literature as well as in the southern counterpart. There is the simplicity of the northern ring as depicted in Eddic literature, but a simplicity that garners beauty through the gold of which it is made. There is also the magic of the northern ring, that is the generic magic that is made possible by the belief in such a marvel. It is, however, the southern concepts that spell out the specifics of that magic, details which -- in turn - give the ring a brilliance, a splendor, and a nobility that make it at once a work of art, a work of beauty, and a work of authority.

Wagner's composite ring was now finished in all ways but one. There remained one last factor that had to be included before the ring of the Nibelung drama could be considered truly completed. This lacking feature was that aspect of the wishing-rod that made its magic operative, that "nature" that one had to know to allow the owner to become that master of the universe. This nature is not divulged in the German poem, and Eddic literature makes no reference to any similar concept. Thus, as Wagner transferred the magic and the power of *Nibelungenlied's* wishing-rod to his ring, it became necessary for him to make his own interpretation of that *nature* that would set the magic of his ring in motion. Wagner's creative mind deigned that this nature, if it was to be accepted dramatically, should relate to a human condition rather than to one that was possible only for divine or supernatural figures. He attempted to draw from what he thought was the basic character of mankind, and perhaps he was also prodded in this endeavor by his own personal domestic experiences. He reasoned, ultimately, that the most valued quality of all life was the love that two mortals could come to know, the love that was experienced when a man and a woman yearned to be united as one by their emotions. He was convinced that there was nothing in the existence of man that could equal such a love, and he deduced that to relinquish it, that is, to surrender love of one's own accord, would be an act that could be prompted only by the belief that there was obtainable in its place something of greater value. At the same time, Wagner was convinced that the urge to control, the urge to have power, the urge to dominate was a vicious lust that was innate in mankind. He felt that this enticement was so infectious that it caused those in whom it had taken root to perform any act, to subscribe to any idea, to relinquish any thing, even love, to have that desire satisfied. Wagner now had the nature that would perfect his ring. The desire to "... master every man in the whole world" would now be cause for the forswearance of love, an inducement to abandon mankind's most sought after ideal, the love and affection of a man and a woman. Wagner brought this 'nature' to his ring, and as he fused this aspect with the other features that he had adapted from the ancient past, he felt that he had now made it complete.

The ring that Wagner brought to his Siegfried drama is exemplary of the manner in which the composer was able to utilize the features of another time into a contemporary dramatic advantage. The ring of his drama, when viewed in its totality and in the light of its dramatic purpose, is really a seamless composite of the major attributes that distinguish each of the several rings of mythical literature. It is apparent that Wagner did not incorporate into the ring of his drama each specific characteristic that early Teutonic thought had attached to its rings, and it is equally apparent that he had created an origin of his own and had adapted a function from separate and distinct items. Yet, there can be no doubt that Wagner was able to cause his ring to be a remarkable reflection of that early culture's prominent concepts of one of Teutondom's most valued and treasured items. His dramatic depiction of the ring, when merged with the role that he gave it in his version of the downfall of the gods, allowed the ring to emerge as a truly exceptional item, one that serves the drama and its figures in a most unique but natural manner, yet an item that readily is an exemplary representation of heathen cultural beliefs.

The ring that Wagner created for his Nibelung tale is something more than simply a replica in form and concept of one of Teutondom's major properties. In the Siegfried drama, the ring that is forged by the Nibelung dwarf Alberich commands a role and a function that are so fundamental to the drama that this unadorned circlet of gold essentially rises to majestic dramatic heights and stands thematically separate and aside from all other items, all figures, and all actions. If Wagner's ring exhibits a mythical authenticity, which it does, it also becomes the story's stimulus for the major theme of *The Ring of the Nibelung*, and therefore the parent also of the several tangential themes as well. Wagner's ring is the sole stimulus, the cause as it were, of all that occurs physically, emotionally, and intellectually in the tale of the gods. Wagner's ring gives rise to greed, and to a lust for domination and power. Wagner's ring stimulates the intense hatreds, the subtle remorse, the wrath, the woe, indeed the tragedy, in which the drama is steeped. However, as this ring of gold sits at the core of Wagner's drama, as all else revolves around it, it is a silent witness as well as a passive participant in all that takes place. Wagner's ring is at once everything and it is everywhere in the drama, and in this multi-faceted role that the composer developed so effectively, this ring acquires an importance and a significance that are unapproached by all else in the poem. This single item carries a total import that is so considerable that Wagner gave it recognition in the most appropriate manner possible: he cited it as part of the master title of his mighty four-part work.

Supplement A

THE ANCIENT TEUTONIC WORLD
AND ITS MYTHOLOGY
- A Summary -

Despite the prominence in history of that society known as *Germanic* or *Teutonic*, there is no single word that satisfactorily denotes the geographic region that became the homeland of that rather large cultural group. This vast expanse of land, which includes most of central Europe, as well as the regions to its north and northwest, was the home of kindred groups and tribes that manifested a culture that was essentially common to all the people. However, despite those cultural elements that stimulated association and relationship among the people, there were several factors that prevented this expanse from becoming a politically unified territory to which an inclusive name could be attached.

In the days of the formation of the culture, it was an unsettled, restive people who inhabited part of the area. There was much activity in the form of movements to different regions, treks that sought a better life, even some explorations, and the adventures of mini-conquests. There was conflict that initiated hostilities, some of which often resulted in wars and invasions. There was also the inevitable regional variations in attitudes and societal conduct. These matters, strengthened by a natural tendency on the part of the people to give names only to local areas of interest and concern, hindered the use of any one word that referred specifically to the entirety of this section of the world.

At one time, there was a term that denoted this territory and which might have become a permanent name for the region. That word was *Germania*, which is the title of a book (c. 98 A.D.) that has proved to be a major source for the early history of the people of the region. This work was written by the Roman historian Tacitus who, in addition to calling the land "Germania," called the people who had settled there *Germani*. This latter word is the earliest-known accepted term that collectively referred to the people of these related groups.

Variations of the original words used by Tacitus remained as part of the English language, but the original meanings fell into disuse and eventually were replaced. In time, the words *Germania* and *Germani* became *Germany* and *Germans*, which in turn were permanently applied to a specific portion of the original territory and to the people who had established themselves there. These words continue to be used in that manner in the modern day. Despite the narrow applications that became the semantic fate of these two related terms with their rather broad initial meanings, there was a companion word with an equally extensive initial concept that did not suffer a reduced meaning and which remained in use as it had developed originally. That word was *Germanic*, a descriptive term that designated *all* the associated people who lived in this vast region, and their way of life, and who, today, are divided into no less than eleven nationalities (Afrikaners, Danish, Dutch, English, Faroese, Fleming, Frisian, German, Icelander, Norwegian, and Swedish).

In addition to the word "Germanic," there is, of course, that second term that is widely used in current English to denote all of the people who are considered native to this total area and those matters associated with them. This second word is *Teutonic*, a term that is derived from *Teuton* or *Teutones*, the name of one of the more populous and more active tribes that settled early in the northern region.

In a very real sense, the term "Teutonic" is a word that has a single basic meaning. Its semantics originally denoted or made references to the people and the matters of a specific tribe or clan, and in that usage it was not a word that included all the people of all the numerous groups that inhabited the Germanic territory. However, the Teutones became a celebrated people, one of the most famed of all the early peoples, and use of their name as a reference to all the people gained a linguistic foothold early in the historical attention to the territory. It was because of this fame and the early references to the tribe that the word "Teutonic" soon was a term of common usage by historians. linguists, mythologists, and other scholars.

The use of the term "Teutonic" has been enhanced by the appearance and acceptance of related words that also were derived from the original *Teuton*. Such words as *Teutonism*, *Teutonist*, and *teutonize* are heard and read with regularity today.

It seems only natural that those interested in a name for the territory in question would turn -- sooner or later -- to the word "Teuton." The English language had never devised its name for the land in question, yet there were several distinct terms that, in one way or another, made references to these people and their way of life, all derived from one source-word. Those who worked with such matters as mythology, history, geography or even religion apparently felt the need for such a geographic name for all these Germanic lands and saw semantic opportunity in the use of the ancient word upon which the other words had been built. Thus, in recent times, students and scholars have tended to use a word which serves more or less adequately as a name for the geographic home of all the Germanic peoples. That word is *Teutondom* which, despite its obvious inaccuracies is the only term of its kind available in current English. Its use in English is now considered an accepted bit of terminology.

Ancient Teutondom encompassed an extensive range of territory. In its apogee, this land was bounded on the north by the southern regions of modern Norway, Sweden, and the islands of the Baltic sea. It stretched northwest to include Iceland. The area extended southward through modern-day Denmark and into the European continent proper, reaching as far south as the Danube River. The western continental boundary of Teutondom was the Rhine River, and the eastern limit became the Vistula, (Wisla) in Poland which flows in a wide curve past Cracow, Warsaw, and Torun, and empties in the Baltic Sea, east of Gdansk.

In the main, historians are generally agreed that the beginning of what was to become Teutondom and the Teutonic peoples came about around

2500 B.C. It was about this time that there began a dispersion of those people who inhabited that region frequently referred to as Eurasia, probably the central steppes or Great Plain of European Russia. A sizeable number of these people made their way into southern Scandinavia and into northern and central Europe where, by 1800 B.C., they had developed what may be called, if only loosely, a societal community.

These people traveled and settled themselves in this territory in relatively small groups, or tribes. Individual settlements tended to remain separated from each other, at times by great distances and at times by natural boundaries. Each group, naturally, was concerned with its own welfare and thus developed its own political and social structure as well as its own methods of protection and security. Despite the geographic separation, the individuality of each group's internal development, and the fact that at times these tribes were in conflict, even war, with each other, they were unified overall by the two major forces necessary for a binding, cultural singleness: They spoke the same language (Proto Indo-European), and they shared a common perspective of life and practiced a similar habit and routine in that life.

The static quality of this life began to change about 1500 B.C. At this time some of the peoples in the south and southeast made their way northward, into Scandinavia. These invaders somehow had developed a more societal way of life, a more cultural society, one that even boasted its own religion replete with its own gods. This importation into Scandinavia of a new way of life was to have a permanent and profound influence on the civilization of the region which not only absorbed this new thought, but actually built upon it. It was during this period that the germination of what centuries later would be called Teutonic mythology was taking place.

About 1000 B.C. some of the tribes in the north began to stir. The people began to move, to branch out. A slow but steady trek southward began, a movement that could continue during the next several hundred years and which ultimately would have an incredible effect on the future life of all Europe. In the third or fourth century before Christ these people were firmly established in the south of Scandinavia, in the islands of the Baltic Sea, on that part of the continent of Europe which is the great, flat plain of north

Germany, between the Rhine and the Vistula. These were the Teutons or Teutones, the people who even at this time were readily recognized as Germanics.

In the course of time, these Teutonic peoples became divided into three major branches, divisions that were determined more by physical movement, or lack of such movement, than by any radical differentiation of cultural thought or tradition.

The initiation of the movement had occurred among those people who originally had established themselves between the Oder and the Vistula. This group, known historically as the Eastern Branch of the Germanic peoples, began to drift toward the Black Sea. Ultimately, they would settle between the Don and the Carpathian Mountains where, by the fourth century after Christ, they had been converted to Christianity. This early conversion effectively separated them from propagation of the heathen Teutonic thought.

A second group of Germanic peoples was known as the Western Branch. These people had moved southward, and by 200 B.C. had reached the Rhine and the Main rivers. Their movement continued and by the first century after Christ they had occupied the territory between modern-day Denmark and southern Germany, at which time some crossed the sea to establish themselves in Britain. It is out of this branch, which turned to Christianity about 800 A.D., that would come the Anglo-Saxons, the Dutch, the Frisians, and the Germans.

The third of these major groups, the Northern Branch, consisted of those people who remained essentially in the original settlement, that is the southern region of the Scandinavian peninsula. Activity and movement among these people would come in later centuries, and then mostly in a westerly direction. Their conversion to Christianity occurred later than that of other Germanics, about 1200 A.D., and it would be from these people that would spring the Danes, Icelanders, Norwegians, and Swedes.

At the time of the original migration from Eurasia, the people had brought the ways of life and thought that had evolved there through the years. In their new home, they were surrounded by a distinct nature and a different geography, and they felt the needs and necessities for change that this nature and this geography demanded. The people slowly experienced changes and a revamping of the mode and manner of their lives.

New patterns of thought began to emerge. Time and separation from the old order asserted their influence in these alterations. An adjusted view of the universe began to take shape. A new persuasion regarding life was developing and there was a persistent concern with the subtle perplexities of that life. These people were interested in the matter of their origin as well as that of the world in which they lived. They recognized a certain order in the total nature about them, a nature which in many ways dominated much of their existence, and they attempted to propose means for that order and to give answers to the questions that arose regarding any irregularities. These people also conceived a divine world in which there was a life greater than their own, a life that was superior to theirs, but which, nevertheless, manifested much that was a reflection of mortal life. The people also perceived those who were privileged to that life, that is, the gods and other supernatural beings who then took their respective places in their world. These people also demonstrated a special interest in the powers that their gods held, and were concerned about the forces that these divine ones exercised in the universe. These early people gave attention to life and its experiences, but they were also interested in the qualities and actions that strengthened -- or weakened -- that life. Their thoughts, in the main, were of their own existence and continuation of that existence, but they also placed emphasis on an afterlife, an existence after death. They also showed a certain anxiety regarding the attainment of that afterlife. Collectively, these interests, these inquiries, these responses, these concerns, this total religious thought and associated beliefs that came to be so much a part of the lives of these ancient people is what is known today as Teutonic mythology.

The numerous concepts that the Teutonic peoples developed were probably the same for all the people, at least in the prehistoric beginning. Their views of the deities, the various supernaturals, along with their functions and their activities, and the numerous rites, rituals, and religious practices apparently satisfied the inner inquisitiveness of all the people. Unfortunately, little is known about this very early religious thought. There are not extant any documents that speak to the matter and neither are there any relics, structures, or other remains of consequence that are helpful in any serious study. However, the revelations that are to be found in several manuscripts that came into existence several centuries later, as well as significant archaeological finds that date after the commencement of history, indicate that without a doubt the numerous deities and the gallery of other figures that we have come to know as the essence of heathen Germanic religious thought had gained their roots and had become ingrained in the total culture quite early in time.

It was natural that the movement, settlement, and other activity that were to occur throughout heathen Teutondom, and especially in continental Europe, during the centuries would occasion changes in this thought. As the clans and tribes became more separated one from the other or as individual clans moved repeatedly from one area to another, and as new surroundings necessitated physical as well as mental and emotional adjustments, the initial religious concepts were faced with challenge. The new communal life demanded modifications. Some tangential matters bowed under this pressure and some practices underwent alteration. Some ritual was modified according to the demands of the new life. Other rites disappeared, and new ones were born. It was not unusual, for example, for a given rite to be carried out by one clan, while another group, only a few miles distance, was completely unaware of the practice. Neither was it rare for one god to enjoy a cult of great intensity in one area, and then to be considered one of the lesser divine beings in another region. Even the initial roster of divine figures and their purposes for being often differed from one region to the next. And, if a god was to be found in the religious thought of several areas, it is most likely that the name varied from region to region because of the linguistic variations that were also common during this period, differences that resulted as distinct languages began to emerge from the single mother tongue, Old Norse.

Mythologists grouped these differences in heathen Teutonic religious thought and manners according to the regions of practice and then recorded their similarities and differences. These scholars uncovered an incredible number of variances that existed in the totality of Germanic beliefs and concepts, but they were agreed that these diversities were relatively minor ones, that they were differences in detail rather than in substance. Ultimately, however, those who studied these matters concluded that there were two major convictions that were distinct enough to be viewed separately. These same scholars were also quick to assert that each of these two entities uniquely complemented the other, that each was a variation of one basic, fundamental thought that had developed early in the prehistory of the Teutonic peoples. Such an evaluation, which since has proved to be without question, acknowledges that *the people of all of ancient heathen Teutondom had been guided and had found religious solace and comfort in a single body of thought, and had worshiped and carried out their rites and rituals essentially in a like manner.*

For lack of an absolute need, the two bodies of early Teutonic thought were not given proper names. Rather, each was named by locating it within the boundaries of Teutondom. Thus, one was called the *Northern* version and the other the *Southern* version. And, they were called "versions" to indicate their relation to the original beliefs that had been developed and accepted throughout all of the Germanic territory. On the whole, the Northern version included those beliefs and practices that were accepted in Norway, Sweden, Iceland, and the greater part of Denmark. In a similar manner, the Southern version was the accepted religious thought in the remainder of Teutondom, that is, the Germanic regions of continental Europe.

The gods that Wagner included in his *Ring* serve as mythological examples of the varied cultural attitudes of the Northern and Southern versions of Teutonic belief, and the figure of the supreme god, Wotan, adequately illustrates the point. This deity, in the main, held first rank throughout heathen Teutondom, yet his cult and his veneration differed from region to region. In some areas, particularly in the Scandinavia, Wotan's knowledge, his powers and his divine favors were often considered to be less formidable than those of Donner, or even those of Froh. In Germany, however, Wotan was at all times and without question the god of highest rank. In the southern region of Teutondom Wotan also exercised his divine forces alone, without aid, and in his own manner, while in the north he frequently was grouped with Donner and Froh as a kind of Teutonic "Trinity" or "Triad." And, depending upon the place and the time, the great god was known by any of several language variations of a name. In the northern part of the Teutonic world this god was called Voden, Vothen, Othur, Othan, Othin, or Odin, the latter being perhaps the most familiar to native speakers of English. In the south, the god was known as Voden, Vodan, Woden, Wodan, Wuodan, Wuoden, Wooden, Weda, or the now celebrated Wotan.

Wagner's use of the term "Wotan" is an example of the composer's resort to the German or southern Teutonic thought. So, too, did he follow the same procedure with his other deities. Thus, we have Fricka, Donner, Froh, and Freia rather than the Scandinavian versions of Frigg, Thor, Freyr, and Freyja. Wagner's intent, both with the names of his *dramatis personae* as well as in the totality of his drama of the *Ring* was to reproduce as much as possible of this early German belief and to retain the German quality and manner to the extent that his talent permitted. To this end the composer attempted to place his gods, and all else of his story, within a framework that reflected the German, or southern, perception of the divine world.

The knowledge and information regarding this Germanic mythology that is available today has been gained mostly from documents that came into existence relatively late in the history of the heathen Teutonic world. The first graphic finds that were relative to this way of thought were simple runic inscriptions. These materials date from about the second century, but are of little value in the study at hand. The first alphabetic writings appeared some three hundred years later. These were writings that emerged from within the Eastern Branch of the Teutonic peoples, those who had migrated into the region of the Black Sea and who had undergone an early conversion to Christianity. The manuscripts produced by these people were fragmentary translations into Gothic of the *Bible* and certain sacred Christian texts, which, obviously, are a treatment of matters that are far-removed from our concern with the ancient Teutonic religious thought.

The pertinent material that came from the Western Branch of the Germanic peoples, those who settled in what is present-day Germany, was sparse, almost non-existent. For whatever reasons, these peoples did not record the details of their early beliefs and persuasion, modified as it was from the initial conviction that was to be had in Scandinavia. Some information was recorded by Roman observers and there is also some data from later ages, that information set down by the early Christian clergy, that give some evidence of relatively minor variations from the original thought. Most of the early German way of thought, therefore, was handed down to later generations not by means of written documents but by means of the oral tradition. This latter body of data was available to Wagner, but only in a cultural sense, and therefore in a limited manner.

The full texture and vigor of what we today call Teutonic mythology was preserved by the northern or Scandinavian branch of the Germanic peoples. These were the people who had remained essentially at home in the northern lands, who had not participated actively in the numerous migrations throughout the ages, who had developed their own great surge of exploration, invasion, and conquest (Age of the Vikings, 800-1100 A.D.), and who had resisted the inroads that Christianity had made in Europe during this lengthy period. These were the people for whom the Teutonic gods not only held sway during the many centuries, but for whom their dominance showed itself in ever-increasing manners and degrees. Yet, at the same time as the gods reigned in their divine ways, advances in the art of writing stirred the scholars and the poets of the day to record matters of concern and thus it was from the writings of this northern group that the bulk of ancient Teutonic religious and societal thought has been gained. It is from these works, the songs, the sagas, the poems, and even the writings of an historical nature, that the world has come to know of Wotan and his divine cohorts, of the dwarves and giants, of Valhalla and Valkyries, and the heroes who aroused the admiration, respect, and even adoration of the people. It is from this body of literary and historic writings that the specifics of early Teutonic belief have been gleaned, and it is essentially from this data and information that Teutonic mythology has been defined and detailed.

Wagner turned to this Nordic literature as he went about the business of preparing his *Ring* argument. He was aware that there was no similar literature that was of German origin, or a literature that was wholly of German content, but he was also aware that the divine and supernatural figures that appeared in this northern writing, as well as their many activities, were not exclusively singular to Scandinavia but had been very much a part of early German thought. And, he also knew that much of what can be called 'German' thought had made its way north and had been incorporated into the writings of these Nordic people. If at times he encountered variances between the northern and southern versions, he would not show undue concern. He knew that in the end, the ambience, the significance, and the import of these gods were universal to all Teutondom, that their essence was valid in his own native land as well as in the north.

Supplement B

THE SOURCES OF THE RING

In 1848 Wagner wrote a short prose piece which, during the next twenty-six years, would be developed into his music-drama *Der Ring des Nibelungen*. This short sketch, which he titled "Der Nibelungen Mythus, als Entwurf zu einem Drama" ("The Nibelung Myth as Sketch for a Drama"), was his initial concept of a thematic arrangement of two completely unrelated themes, both drawn from Germany's cultural history. One of the themes would concern the legendary Siegfried, the popular national hero whose exploits had been in tales that had been passed down from generation to generation by means of the oral tradition and recorded in numerous medieval lays and songs. The other of the two themes focused on the hierarchy of gods and supernaturals that had dominated the heathen Teutonic world since the earliest of times and whose activities had found their way into prose and poetry in the twelfth and thirteenth centuries.

Wagner's "Sketch" was not the result of an impetuous urge to create. Although it was to undergo much change and alteration before it became the libretto for his *Ring*, this "Sketch" came into existence only after the composer had spent the years 1840-1848 devoted to the study of his country's cultural traditions as well as its dramatic, legendary, mythical, and historical past. He had dug deeply into the Nibelung legend, which had been and remains today one of the most beloved tales in Germany. And his fascination and attraction to myth, coupled with his belief that myth was the only means by which drama could express *basic truth* and manifest the *purely human*, had led him to the nature of Wotan, Fricka and their colleagues. His union of these two worlds by means of a story of his own was unique.

Wagner never discussed at any length the materials that had served as his sources in the preparation of the *Ring* drama. Neither did he offer any details in the numerous essays that he wrote concerning this work. It would seem that the composer assumed that his German public would be so familiar with the cultural aspects of his mythological tale that no discussion or listing of these sources was needed.

There is preserved, however, one short writing in which Wagner was rather specific regarding those works that had served him best in his composition of the *Ring* poem. This writing is a letter written by the composer in response to an inquiry made by Franz Müller, the Court Councillor at Weimar and a Wagner enthusiast. Müller had written a favorable piece on *Lohengrin* and in 1853 Wagner had presented him with a copy of one of the fifty copies of the *Ring* poem that the composer had published at his own expense that year. Müller read the drama, was intrigued by the story that Wagner had created, and ultimately determined that he would do a book on this fascinating tale. Three years later, in June, 1856, Müller wrote Wagner requesting that the composer supply him with the information about the sources that he had consulted. In his response, Wagner cited as his sources eight works and the studies of two scholars. The works were:

        a.   *Edda Saemundar*

        b.   *Volsungasaga*

        c.   *Nibelungen Noth und die Klage*

        d.   *Wilkinasaga*

        e.   *Deutsche Mythologie*

        f.   *Die deutsche Heldensage*

        g.   *Deutsches Heldenbuch*

        h.   *Heimskringla*

and the scholars were:

        i.   Franz Josef Mone

        j.   Karl Lachmann

Of the literature that Wagner had named in his letter to Müller, there were three titles whose contents had served him more thoroughly and more profoundly than the others. These volumes, which may be termed "principal" or "primary" sources, were the recorded versions of the myths and legends that had long existed in oral tradition and which had passed from generation to generation among the Germanic peoples. It would be from these writings that he could actually draw most of the figures of his *dramatis personae*, and find inspiration for those that he himself created. It would also be in these writings that Wagner would find much of the principal action and many of the major items that he would bring into his argument. It would also be in these works that he would find the mythical perspective which he deemed so important, and with which he could put into action his gods and his heroes.

The most important of these primary works is that one which Wagner listed simply as "the *Edda*." This work, whose literary title is *Edda Saemundar*, is recognized throughout the world as the repository of Teutonic mythology. This book, popularly known as *The Poetic Edda* and frequently called *The Elder Edda*, is a collection of some thirty-five poems of varying length, with occasional pieces of short prose interspersed. (The number of poems contained in any edition of the *Edda* depends literally on how an editor divides the stanzas of a series, or possibly joins two or more series of stanzas into a single poem.) These poems, called *lays*, were recorded in Old Norse in Iceland during the second half of the twelfth century and are the written versions of the oral poetry that contained the ancient northern Teutonic peoples' concept of the universe, that is, its origin, its inhabitants, its systems, and its values.

There are two types of lays in *The Poetic Edda*. The first fourteen comprise the section known as "Lays of the Gods." These are the stanzas that present the pantheon of Teutonic deities and other divine and supernatural figures, along with their activities within the Germanic order of the universe. It is in these lays that Wagner found, among other things, his Wotan, his Valkyries, his Valhalla, and the Teutonic concept of the doom and destruction of the universe. The remaining twenty-one poems are grouped under the title "Lays of the Heroes," and contain the heroic lore of the Germanic peoples. Among the major figures in these lays is that of Siegfried, the Volsung. The figures and activities that are present in the first section of the *Edda* are unrelated, either historically or literarily, to those of the companion section and it is in this regard that one of Wagner's more engaging artistic accomplishments is to be noted. Despite this fact that the "Lays of the Gods" and the "Lays of the Heroes" are ancient Teutonic poetry with no thematic relation, Wagner was quite successful in extracting from each of the divisions numerous figures, certain property items, incidents, and themes which he then fused and blended into an original argument that projected the idea and ambience of a single, unified tale of consistent dramatic interplay. That argument was, of course, *The Ring of the Nibelung.*

The fundamental importance of *The Poetic Edda* to Wagner cannot be overstated. Those who are familiar with both the *Edda* and the *Ring* are unquestionably aware of how extensively the composer drew from the *Edda* not only the major mythological aspects that are to be found in his drama, but also much that constitutes the total mythical environment in which the poem is set.

The second of Wagner's primary sources is one of the more prominent of the numerous sagas that came out of the Nordic regions of the Teutonic peoples, the *Volsungasaga* or *Saga of the Volsungs.* This anonymously written Icelandic work, completed around the middle of the thirteenth century, recounts the story of the Volsung clan, with emphasis on the activities of Siegfried, the posthumous son of Siegmund. Overall, this saga is a prose paraphrase of certain poems that are found in *The Poetic Edda*, although there are segments of the story that were developed from other Old Norse poetry. Wagner found in this saga more elaborate versions of certain of the Eddic poems that had inspired his story line, and he also found distinct thematic matters that he was to bring to the *Ring*. At the same time, *Volsungasaga* offered to the composer an intangible consideration that was of great value as he pondered the nationalistic character that he wished his drama to have. If indeed his argument was based essentially on the Nordic version of the mythology and the Siegfried legend, *Volsungasaga* afforded a flavoring of the medieval romanticism that was more southern, that is, more German than Nordic. It was in *Volsungasaga* that Wagner also found the colorful southern heroic values. And, the story in this saga took place in an environment that reflected more the traditions of the culture of the people of the great migration than those of the people who had established a society in the northern regions of Teutondom.

The third of the works that was of primary importance to Wagner and his *Ring* drama was the only of his principal sources that was wholly of German origin. Initially, this lengthy poem carried the title *Nibelung Noth und die Klage* (*Fall of the Nibelungs*), but in time the work became more popularly known as *Nibelungenlied*, or *Song of the Nibelungs*. This poem, which was written anonymously early in the thirteenth century, ultimately came to be considered the national epic of the German people, a distinction that obviously was of some interest to Wagner. The initial import of *Nibelungenlied* to the composer, however, was not its national renown, but rather its story, which was the southern version of what is known as the Nibelung tragedy as it had been orally transmitted in Germany through the years. And, of that story, Wagner's interest lay only in the first of its two parts. The first segment of *Nibelungenlied* relates the activities of Siegfried, Brünnhilde, and Grimhild and ends with the death of the hero. Part two of the work tells of Grimhild's persistent attempt to avenge the murder of her husband, Siegfried.

Die Klage (*The Mourning*) is a short poem that is not a part of the original epic. It was composed by an unknown poet as a means of satisfying the desire for a continuation of the Nibelung story. Written in rhymed couplets and placed at the end of the parent-piece, the poem relates how the survivors at Etzel's court mourned for the heroes who fell to Grimhild's warriors. This work, which is seldom included in any edition of *Nibelungenlied*, was of no source-value to Wagner and his *Ring*.

Wagner had turned to *Nibelungenlied* for certain thematic details, but he also sought other matters of equal if not greater significance in the preparation of his *Ring*. He felt that this work, as a national artwork, was an expression of the nature of the German people, a reflection of those qualities intrinsic in the German character. Wagner sincerely believed that *Song of the Nibelungs* depicted the virtue, the pride, the honor, and the strength of the German culture. He sensed also that from the work he had learned of his culture's basic substance, and of the tone and coloring that stood it apart from other cultures. From *Nibelungenlied* he believed that he had been able to garner the essence that permitted him a fuller and more profound understanding of the core of German thought. Since he was intent on creating a work that bespoke the fundamental greatness of his nation, it was natural, then, that *Nibelungenlied* serve as inspiration for his dramatic depiction of the German spirit.

Wagner also read with interest a fourth literary work which, if of less than primary importance to him and his development of the *Ring* argument, was nevertheless significant in a subtle manner. This work was *Wilkinasaga* (*Vilkina Saga*), often called *Thidrekssaga* (*Dietrich's Saga*). (The name "Wilkina," taken from one of the saga's sections, was given to the saga as a name by the work's first editor.) This thirteenth-century work includes numerous legends, most of which were derived from German poems taken into Norway by migrants and written down by an anonymous Icelander. One of these many tales is that of the hero Theodoric (Thidrek) the Great, known in German as Dietrich von Bern, during his stay in the court of Attila. This is the same Dietrich who appears in *Nibelungenlied* and who conquers Siegfried's murderer and delivers him to the hero's widow, Grimhild.

The value of *Wilkinasaga* to Wagner was that work's presentation of what may be called the *German heroic tradition*. He had little dramatic concern for the figures of this saga, or their actions, but he was attracted to the protagonist in whom he saw a representation of the German concept of the exemplary hero. Dietrich was the fearless, noble leader, an honorable man who embodied the southern (German) code of heroic conduct. This was the characterization and these were the attributes that he wished to bring to his Siegfried and *Thidrekssaga* became an inspirational font for such a portrayal.

The remaining literary works, including the studies of Mone and Lachmann, were indeed source works to Wagner for his preparation of the *Ring* libretto, but they served in a manner different from that of those works that have been discussed. These secondary works did not provide Wagner with matters directly related to the argument of his drama, but rather they opened to him the sum and substance that could best be used to create the dramatic environment in which his story could unfold. Wagner found in

Jakob Grimm's *Deutsche Mythologie* an authoritative and primary source for the study of any facet of German mythology. In *Die deutsche Heldensage*, written by Wilhelm Grimm, Jakob's brother, the composer was able to familiarize himself with the story line of numerous German heroic and epic tales and thus gain a greater insight into the national concept. (These are the Grimm brothers who collaborated in the publication of a book of fairy tales that became celebrated around the world.) The six volumes of *Deutsches Heldenbuch* was essentially a treasure of German medieval poetry that contributed greatly to Wagner's comprehension of the foundations of the German culture and spirit. The Icelander Snorri Sturluson authored the work titled *Heimskringla* which was an attempt to present the broad and balanced history of the kings of Norway. Wagner had no direct interest in the history that this work presented, but he was drawn to the numerous references and details of a mythological nature, and he was fascinated by the Teutonic ambience that saturated the work. Wagner reread this work several times before his death.

Franz Josef Mone and Karl Lachmann were recognized scholars of German literature. Each had studied fields related to heroic and epic literature and each had published tracts and monographs that could have served Wagner in his persistent quest for Teutonic authenticity. Mone's primary interest lay in the area of the history of German literature, with an emphasis on the heroic sagas and the pre-Christian culture. Lachmann was concerned primarily with *Nibelungenlied* and its origin, and it was he who first proposed that the German epic was not a single poem by one author, but rather a collection of twenty songs or lays joined together by appropriate connective poetry. This theory was not discounted until after his death.

These, then, were the sources that Wagner cited as his sources for the *Ring*. As evidenced by this list of works and scholars, there is every indication that Wagner had versed himself in his country's history, myth, and legend in a most sound manner. As evidenced by his *Ring* drama, it is quite certain that Wagner learned his subject well.

Supplement C

TEUTONIC MYTHOLOGY - SOME SPECIFICS

The primary sources that served Richard Wagner in his creation of *The Ring of the Nibelung* were writings that originated, in the main, in northern Teutondom. These works, complemented only infrequently by the sparse writings of the southern peoples, allowed him access to the fundamental concepts of the universe and all within it that were held throughout the heathen Teutonic world. He was aware that there were some minor variations of this thought from region to region, but he encountered no serious difficulties as he wove numerous details, figures, events, actions, concepts, and cultural attitudes into the complex but cohesive dramatic tapestry that was to be the *Ring*.

The same sources that Wagner used to develop the argument of his drama are also those that became the basis for the studies of this volume. In the preparation of these essays, it became obvious early on that certain aspects of ancient Teutonic thought, as depicted in the sources, were common to more than one of the individual subject matters. Such a situation forewarned of repetition of the bulk of numerous details in several essays. Such repetition, regardless of how pertinent or significant any data may be, would not only weaken any continuity or consistency of these studies, but would also constitute monotony, even boredom, for the guiltless reader. Some appropriate means had to be devised to offset those distracting possibilities while at the same time allowing ready availability of certain pertinent mythological matters.

The following arrangement seemed to offer the most advantageous manner to avoid, as much as possible, the potential problem of repetition of material. When a mythological matter is pertinent to more than one chapter of this volume, limited but pertinent data and information will be included in the respective chapters. Then, an asterisk (*) will be placed at an appropriate place in the discussion. For each item so marked, a more complete presentation will be found in this *Supplement*.

THE RELATIONSHIP OF THE GODS

The relationship of the gods that Wagner included in the *Ring* argument is, for the most part, one of his own creation, and therefore differs somewhat from that found in the myths. The composer presents Wotan and Fricka as husband and wife. Donner, Freia, Fricka, and Froh are brothers and sisters, and Loge is cousin to the lot.

The union of Wotan and Fricka as husband and wife is an accurate presentation of the beliefs that were prevalent throughout all of Teutondom. It is obvious, however, that Wagner felt no dramatic or thematic compulsion to include in his poem, either by reference or inference, any of the children that were born to this pair, not even the most beloved of gods, Balder.

The foremost brother-sister relationship among the Teutonic deities is that of Froh and Freia. These two were the children of Njord, and originally were deities of the Vanir (Wanes), a race of gods that had developed in the region of the Baltic Sea. It was the Vanir who had waged what is known as *The First War* against the Aesir gods of which Wotan was the supreme god. Wotan used his famed spear against the Vanir who were no match for the Aesir. As part of the pact that was concluded between the two races of gods, Froh and Freia became hostages of the Aesir, in exchange for Honir and Mimir. This brother-sister pair was accepted into the Aesir race and became two of the most prominent deities of the Teutonic peoples, especially in Scandinavia.

In Germanic beliefs, Donner was not related to Froh or Freia, and he had only an indirect relationship with Fricka. The God of Thunder was the son of Wotan and Iord (Earth) and the second god, after his father, in cult and veneration. By some standards, Donner was the stepson of Fricka, but such a relationship is unheralded and unimportant in Teutonic mythology.

Loge's relationship in the *Ring* as a cousin to the four gods is one that Wagner created. This relationship is mentioned in the drama in only a passing manner and it is of no real consequence in the development of the argument. However, Wagner's Loge was, like the figure that was so consistently present in the early Teutonic mind, a wily, shrewd being who travels among the gods and who is generally the cause of much strife and discord among the Aesir clan. Loge is usually tolerated by the gods, in the *Ring* as well as in the mythology, and in both he is also a frequent companion to Wotan.

RAGNARÖK

Ancient Germanic thought held that the world was destined to ultimate doom and total destruction. The term that was used to designate this fate was *ragnarök*, a compound word that consisted of the terms *ragna* and *rök*. In the compound form, *ragna* is the genitive plural of the word 'power,' a word that was synonymous with 'god.' The word *rök* can be translated as 'fate' or 'doom.' Thus, *ragnarök* meant "fate (doom) of the powers (gods)."

The term *ragnarök*, in time, became involved in some linguistic confusion. The pronunciation of the suffix *rök* was interchanged with that of *rökkr*, a word that meant 'dusk' or 'darkness.' Thus *ragnarökkr* was translated as "dusk (darkness) of the gods." This confusion permitted Wagner to draw from *ragnarök* for much in his *Ring* drama and from *ragnarökkr* he gained a title of one of the drama's four parts.

The Teutonic peoples believed that the gods would be the cause of the end of the universe. If, in a sense, these gods of Teutondom exhibited a certain conviviality among themselves, there was within them the seeds of their own destruction. Mythological thought held that a latent corruption flowed in the blood of the supreme god, Wotan, and that corruption would one day cause the world to be plagued by powerful forces of destruction which, in due time, would erupt.

The end of the world, the *ragnarök*, begins in a rather subtle manner. Wotan has made a pact with a giant, a pact that he later breaks. The god's action was one of the two most serious crimes of the Teutonic world. (The other was *murder*.) Wotan's falseness causes dishonesty to become a factor in divine life. Soon, the gods begin to show distrust for each other. Quarrels erupt. Disagreement and dissension become rampant as deep hostilities develop. Conflicts are numerous. At the same time, murder, even fratricide, is frequently committed. Lasciviousness among the gods becomes widespread. Incest and infidelity are common practices.

The physical aspects of *ragnarök* begin with the death of the god Balder. This son of Wotan and Fricka was the purest, the wisest, and the most respected figure of all the gods. His death, which comes about through the trickery and deceit of Loge, causes much sorrow and grief among the gods. Wotan even begets a son who, on the day after his birth, attempts to avenge his brother's murder.

After Balder's death, the universe of the gods experiences a series of major disruptions. The river Slih ("Fearful") rises in the Land of the Giants and begins to overflow its banks. The dwarves who live in the bowels of the earth become restless and apprehensive. The dead in Hel begin to stir. Nature erupts in a full fury of unending snows and great blizzards. There is frost and cold and biting winds everywhere and the warmth of the sun cannot be felt. The wolf Skoll chases the sun, catches her, and then swallows her. Hati, another wolf, steals the moon from the heavens. The cock Fjalar then crows to awaken the giants who, since their deception at the hands of Wotan, have been the enemies of the gods. Garm, the guard dog at the gates of Hel, begins to howl mournfully, and Gollinkambi, the cock, crows to awaken the gods and Wotan's army of slain heroes in Valhalla. The world serpent Jormungander, more popularly known as Midgardsorm, twists and coils in the oceans and the spirits of the waters begin to writhe in the depths. The World Ash Tree shakes and shivers. The gods are beset with anxiety; they meet in council and Wotan seeks guidance from the severed head of Mimir, the wise spirit who once had been the guardian of the Spring of Wisdom and to whom Wotan long ago had given an eye for a drink of the spring's water.

The situation in the universe has become so tense that the only recourse for the gods is to stand and face their enemies in The Final Battle.

In this violent last conflict, Wotan and the other deities die, after which the world also suffers its cataclysmic final moments. First, the sun turns black, and the stars lose their light. Then, the earth begins to tremble, mountains shake and crash to bits, and the heavens are torn apart. The world is shattered and bursts into flames. The fire spreads, engulfs the earth, and then reaches into the heavens. The waters of the seas now swell, overflow, and flood the earth which then slowly sinks into the watery depths amid a great swirl of smoke and hissing steam.

The end is at hand. The destruction of the major gods and the universe that they had governed is complete. *Ragnarök*, the 'twilight of the gods,' *Götterdämmerung* has been realized.

THE FINAL BATTLE

As the name implies, The Final Battle is that last armed conflict before the universe comes to its inglorious but predestined end. The great and powerful gods of Teutondom will meet their doom in this battle, after which the corrupt universe that they had created will be destroyed in *ragnarök*.

In the first stages of the conflict the enemies of the gods move to confront their foes. The giant Hrym captains a ship that carries the giants that will do combat with the gods. The dead of Hel sail out on a ship that has Loge at its helm. Fenrir, father of Skoll and Hati and offspring of Loge, advances, followed by wild men. Surt and his army of fire-giants prepare to cross Bifrost, the Rainbow Bridge that serves as entrance to the Land of the Gods. The world serpent emerges from the ocean spewing venom far and wide.

The gods prepare themselves for combat. When Heimdall, the sentry for the gods and the guardian of the Rainbow Bridge, sees the approaching enemy, he sounds an alert on his horn Gjallarhorn ("Shrieking Horn"). Wotan hears the warning sound and with his army of fallen warriors behind him, he leaves Valhalla to do battle in the conflict that will herald the end of the universe.

The great battle takes place on the vast plain of Vigrid (Field of Battle) that stretches out before Valhalla. It is there that the gods, the fire-giants, the frost-giants, the dead, and the monsters of the world will meet in battle. Wotan attacks Fenrir who feeds on the dead and then besmears the god's home with blood. The wolf kills the god, and then swallows him. To avenge his father's death, Wotan's son Vidar then attacks and slays the wolf. Donner advances on the World Serpent and kills him. However, the God of Thunder is overcome by the serpent's venom and after walking nine steps, he falls dead. Froh attacks Surt, the leader of the fire-giants, and falls in battle. Heimdall and Loge slay each other. Hraesvelg, the eagle that had sat in the World Ash Tree and had created the wind with his wings, flies down to the field of battle and there gnaws on screaming corpses. As the din and struggle of battle subside, the world begins to collapse, and *ragnarök*, "the twilight of the gods", is upon the universe. The end is exactly as the high-seeress had predicted.

THE NINE WORLDS

The heathen Teutonic peoples believed that the universe consisted of nine distinct worlds, each inhabited by a special kind of being. These worlds were housed within Yggdrasil, the Teutonic 'tree of life' which is also known as the World Ash Tree.

These nine worlds were:

1. Jotunheim - The Land of the Giants
2. Alfheim - The Land of the Elves
3. Muspellsheim - The Land of the Fire-Giants
4. Svartalfaheim - The Land of the Dark Elves
5. Niflheim - The Land of the Dead
6. Asgard - The Land of the Aesir Gods
7. Vanaheim - The Land of the Vanir Gods
8. Midgard - The World of Men
9. Nidavellir (?) - The World of the Dwarves
   (There is some question about the existence of this mythical world.)

Some scholars of the religions of the world have related the heathen concept of nine worlds with the concept of the five worlds that exist in Christian beliefs: Earth, Heaven, Hell, Limbo, and Purgatory.

RUNES

The runes of the ancient Germanic peoples, and their functions, were a distinctive feature of that early culture. A rune, represented by a visible sign or mark, was an instrument of charm and magic that accounted for many of the religious rites, rituals, and cultural practices that developed and persisted throughout Teutondom.

The Old Norse word for 'rune' was *run*, which meant literally *mystery* or *secret* in the sense of *mysterious secret* or *mysterious knowledge*. It was through these meanings that runes were thought to be the wisdom of the world and to contain the secret of all things. Thus it was that the runes exerted a unique influence and control over the behavioral patterns of the people. The concept of the rune and its powers was so imbedded and so widespread throughout Teutondom that it was preserved in England until the seventeenth century and remains evident in modern German culture through the word *raunen* ("to whisper").

In its simplest form, a rune was a special mark that was orally identified by a sound. Today, those sounds or proto-sounds serve as the names of the runes. There was, for example, the Old Norse rune ᚱ whose proto-sound was *fehu* and which was the rune for the god Froh. Another Old Norse rune was ᚾ, whose proto-sound was *naudir* and which was the rune for *naud* ("need"). In later times these two runes became equated with the letters *F* and *N* respectively. The visual design of each rune was relatively uncomplicated, usually a combination of vertical and horizontal lines. In the beginning, the runes were carved into wood, but in time they were scratched, occasionally engraved, into stone, metal, bone, and animal horn. Originally, there were twenty-four runes (the Germanic runes) which date from about 250-150 B.C. After their introduction into Scandinavia, they were reduced in number to sixteen. (In Old English, the number of runes became thirty-three.)

The runic marks were never intended as a means for practical communication. Rather, these signs were utilized as symbols to denote some mysterious secret, a special essence or authority which each rune reputedly was capable of realizing. In the minds of the people, each rune was possessed of certain magical powers, charmed forces or energy that allowed specific tangible results to be achieved. The belief in the powers of runes was so extensive and so profound throughout the Teutonic world that the ends gained through their use sometimes bordered on the miraculous. It was believed, for example, that runes could be used to kill, or to prevent death, or to bring back life. There were runes that were used to heal as well as to make ill. Others were used to extinguish fires, to calm stormy seas, to make needed rain fall from the skies. Runes were also used to advance or delay a birth, to spoil a crop, to make a weapon strong or weak, to bind thieves, to call up evil spirits. There were also runes for love, battle, fertility, thought and speech. (Each rune was supposedly capable of realizing several distinct acts.) In short, the people believed that through the use of runes almost any act or action, whether divine, human, or natural, could be realized, or in some cases prevented.

Runes had to be "worked" to be effective. In order for the magic of any rune to be brought into action, the rune had to have a "correct interpretation." Each rune was different and the acts necessary to bring about the powers of the rune were likewise different. At times, simple incantations could be used. Other runes required elaborate rituals before their magic could be brought to bear. Once the rune had been "worked" properly and the "correct interpretation" achieved, its powers could be stopped only by the figure who had cast the rune. When a rune became operative, the user then usually inscribed its mark on some object.

The ability to work runes so that a special result was realized was considered a "gift." It was believed that the gods, because they were divine, were capable of bringing all the powers of all the runes into action. Wotan had such control of the runes and was so adept in their use that one of his many names was "Lord of the Runes." It was also believed that some mortals had received the "gift" from the gods and had learned the treasured secret of some of the runes. These special persons, then, could bring into action the forces of the runes which they controlled. Such persons were relatively few in number and therefore were looked upon as beings of special favor, persons who were to be courted as well as feared by the society in which they lived.

Runes were a predominant feature of the heathen practices of the early Germanic peoples. The belief in and use of runes continued in the southern Teutonic world well after the introduction of Christianity in the eighth century. In the northern Teutonic world, where Christianity did not arrive until the twelfth century, runes were still a part of the culture for another four hundred years.

INDEX

A

AEGISHJALMR,
Helm of Terror, 47-48

AESIR,
Pact with a giant, 79;
The First War, 53, 79;
Wotan's race of gods, 24, 134

AFRIKANER,
Teutonic peoples, 114

ALBERICH,
A Nibelung, 98;
Fashions a ring, 51;
Guardian of Nibelung
treasure, 46;
Initial theft of gold, 65;
Tarnhelm, 42;
Tarnkappe, 46;
Urge to rule the world, 109;
Utters death-curse, 108

ALFHEIM,
Land of the Elves, 138

ALLFATHER,
See: WOTAN

ANDHRIMNIR,
Chef to the gods, 75

ANDVARANAUT,
Andvari's ring, 105-107

ANDVARI,
A dwarf, 43;
Owns Andvaranaut,
105-106;
Utters death-curse,
106, 108

ANDVARI'S GEM,
Andvari's ring, 106

ANGLO-SAXON,
Western Branch of Teutonic
peoples, 117

ANIMAL,
Guard dog in Hel, 136;
In *Ring*, 4, 8;
In World Ash Tree, 16;
Sacrifice, 8;
Sign of war, 12;
See also:
BEAR
BOAR
DEER
DOG
DRAGON
EAGLE
FALCON
FINCH
GOAT
HART
HAWK
HORSE
OTTER
OXEN
PIG
RAVEN
ROOSTER
SALMON
SERPENT
SHEEP
SQUIRREL
SWAN
TOAD
WOLF

ANVIL,
Cleaved in two, 89, 91

APPLE,
Chapter II, 63-70;
Freia as guardian, 66-68;
"Golden" apples, 69;
Idun abducted, 65;
Idun as guardian, 27, 66;
In *Ring*, 64-65;

APPLE (*Cont*),
Mythical magic,
65-66, 68-69;
Societal importance, 63;
Wagner's adaptations, 69-70;
Wagner's thoughts on, 63-64

ASABRU,
Bridge of the Aesir Gods
(Rainbow Bridge), 24

ASES,
Aesir gods, 79

ASGARD,
Built by the gods, 71;
Hel cannot invade, 75;
Land of the Gods,
17, 25, 78, 138;
Location of Valhalla, 74;
Rebuilt by a giant, 79-80;
Suffers much during
The First War, 79

ASH (Tree),
As charcoal, 13-14;
Askr Yggdrasil, 15;
Associated with Wotan,
13, 15, 18;
Association with a wolf, 13;
Chapter II, 7-22;
First mortal man, 8;
For spears, 13;
Hunding's tree, 14;
In myth, 12-13;
Sign of good luck, 86;
Tree of war, 13;
World Ash Tree, 4

ASH STEED OF YGG,
Wotan, 15

ASK,
First mortal man, 8

ASPEN (Tree),
In *The Poetic Edda*, 11

ATLI,
Nordic name for ATTILA
(q.v.)

ATTILA,
Atli, 103;
Etzel, 88;
Father of Gutrune's two
children, 103;
His death foreseen, 104;
King of the Huns, 88;
Weds Gutrune, 107;
Wilkinasaqa, 130

AXE,
A weapon of war, 83

B

BALDER,
A god, Wotan's favorite son,
36, 75, 104;
Consecrated by Mjollnir,
36, 104;
Gives Draupnir to Hermod,
105;
His death, 43, 75, 104, 134;
Hod, his brother, 75;
In *ragnarök*, 136;
Mistletoe, 75;
Most beloved of the gods,
134;
Raised after death, 36, 75

BALDER'S DREAM,
An Eddic poem, 104

BALLAD OF RIG, THE,
An Eddic poem, 26

BALLAD OF SKIRNIR, THE,
An Eddic poem, 69

BALLAD OF
THE HIGH ONE, THE,
An Eddic poem,
18, 59

BALMUNG,
Description, 93;
Hagen takes, 93;
How Wagner used, 96;
Presented to Siegfried, 93;

BALMUNG *(Cont)*,
Siegfried's sword
(*Nibelungenlied*), 88;
Used to slay Hagen, 95;
See also:
GRAM
NOTUNG
SWORD

BALTIC SEA,
Teutonic region, 115

BATTLE, THE FINAL,
Depiction, 138;
Donner and World Serpent
fight, 37;
Fire-Giants prepare for,
24-25;
Giants will attack gods, 80;
Heimdall and Loge
fight, 26;
Ragnarök, 16, 20, 137-138;
Takes place on Vigrid, 75;
The sword, 86;
Wotan and Fenrir fight,
54, 86;
Wotan's army to fight, 76

BEAR,
In *Ring*, 4

BEECH (Tree),
In *The Poetic Edda*, 11

BEGINNING, THE,
See: CREATION

BELT,
Donner's, 31

BIFROST,
Nordic name for the
Rainbow Bridge (q.v.)

BILROST,
Nordic name for the
Rainbow Bridge (q.v.)

BILSKIRNIR,
Donner's home, 78

BIRCH (Tree),
Drink of Forgetfulness, 11

BITER,
A sword, 86

BLACKENED, THE,
Boar eaten in Valhalla
(Saehrimnir), 75

BLACK SEA,
Eastern Branch of Teutonic
peoples, 117

BLAIN,
A giant in Creation, 86

BLOOD SNAKE,
A sword, 86

BOAR,
Food in Valhalla, 54, 63, 75;
Gullinbursti, 32, 104;
In *Ring*, 8

BOLVERK,
Wotan, 45

BORGHILD,
Murders Sinfjotli, 98;
Siegmund's first wife, 90

BRAGI,
God of Poetry, 103;
Idun's husband, 66

BRANSTOCK,
Hunding's tree, 14-15;
Wotan thrusts sword
into, 89;
See also: OAK

BRIDGE,
See: RAINBOW BRIDGE

BRIDGE OF THE AESIR GODS,
Asabru (Rainbow Bridge),
24

BRIMIR,
A giant in Creation, 86

BRITAIN,
Western Teutonic region,
117

BROKK,
A dwarf, 32;
Donner's hammer, 33, 104;
Fashions Froh's boar,
32-33, 104;
Forges Wotan's ring, 33,
104-105

BRÜNNHILDE,
A mortal, 64;
A shield maid, 103;
Her wisdom, 10;
Overpowered by Siegfried,
46, 107;
Queen of Isenland, 46;
Receives Andvaranaut as
gift, 107, 108;
To take Siegmund to
Valhalla, 80;
Valkyrie, 10, 22

BRYNY,
Part of Fafner's treasure, 48

C

CARPATHIAN MOUNTAINS,
Teutonic boundary, 117

CAULDRON ROARING,
A spring (Hvergelmir),
16, 74

CHAMPIONS (Warriors),
Drink special mead, 74;
Einherjar, 72;
Life in Valhalla, 76;
Sintolt the Hegeling, 80;
Those chosen, 80;
Transported to Valhalla by
Valkyries, 80;
Wittig the Irming, 80

CHANGING, THE,
Wotan, 45

CHARCOAL,
Ash, 13-14

CHARMS,
Drink of Forgetfulness, 11;
In drink, 10;
Linden tree, 12;
Runes, 139-141;
The sword, 84;
See also: MAGIC

CHILD OF NEED,
Notung, 98

CHOOSERS OF THE SLAIN,
Valkyries, 76

CHRISTIANITY,
Conversion of Eastern
Teutonic peoples, 117;
Conversion of Western
Teutonic peoples, 117;
Christian Cross and
Donner's hammer, 37;
Five worlds, 139;
In Scandinavia, 122;
Runes, 141

CLIFF OF HEAVEN,
Heimdall's home, 25

CLOAK OF DISGUISE,
Tarnkappe, 45

CLUB,
A weapon of war, 83

COCK,
See: FJALAR
GOLLINKAMBI

COMPASS POINTS,
In Ring, 4

CORD OF DESTINY,
Woven by Norns, 19, 20

CORD OF FATE,
See: CORD OF DESTINY

CRACOW (Poland),
Teutonic boundary, 115

CREATION,
Blain, 86;
Brimir, 86;
Dwarfs, 86;
Of the Universe, 71;
Of the World of Man, 7-8

CREMATION,
Balder and Nanna, 36, 105

CRUSHER,
Donner's hammer,
See: MJOLLNIR

CURSE,
Alberich's death-curse, 108;
Andvari's death-curse,
106, 108

D

DANISH,
A Prince, 88;
Teutonic peoples, 114, 117

DANUBE,
Teutonic boundary, 115

DARK BITER, THE,
A serpent, 16

DAUGHTER-IN-LAW,
See: SNOR

DEATH,
Alberich's curse of death,
108;
Andvari's curse of death,
106;
Beginning of *ragnarök*, 136;
Entry into Valhalla, 72;
Land of the Dead, 72;

DEATH *(Cont),*
Place to which cadavers are
consigned, 72;
Siegfried's death, 93

DEER,
In *Ring*, 4

DENMARK,
King Hunding, 90;
Part of Northern religious
thought, 120;
Teutonic region, 115, 117;
See also: DANISH

DESTINY,
See: CORD OF DESTINY

DESTROYER,
Donner's hammer,
See: MJOLLNIR

DESTRUCTION,
Siegfried's sword,
See: BALMUNG

DEUTSCHE HELDENSAGE, DIE,
Source for the *Ring*,
126, 130-131

DEUTSCHE MYTHOLOGIE,
Source for the *Ring*,
126, 130-131

DEUTSCHES HELDENBUCH,
Source for the *Ring*,
126, 130-131

DIENSTAG,
Tuesday, 85

DIETRICH (Thidrek, Theodoric),
Fights Hagen, 94;
German hero, 88;
Wilkinasaga, 130

DISGUISE,
See: TRANSFORMATION

DOG,
See: GARM

DON (River),
Teutonic boundary, 117
DONNER,
Associated with oak tree,
11, 15;
Clears away mists, 23;
Compared with Heimdall,
26-27;
Fights World Serpent,
37, 138;
Halfdan, a son, 31;
His belt, 31;
His gloves, 31;
His hammer, Chapter IV,
31-39;
His home, 78;
His wife, 32;
Killed in The Final Battle,
138;
Member of Triad,
27, 120-121;
One of five gods in *Ring*, 66;
Other sons, 37;
Relationship in *Ring*,
134-135;
Slays a giant, 80;
Threatens Fafner
and Fasolt, 56;
Threatens Loge, 34;
Threatens Wotan, 34

DONNER'S HAMMER,
See: MJOLLNIR

DRAGON,
Fafner, 47, 106; .
Guards a treasure, 88;
In *Ring*, 4, 13;
See also: FAFNER

DRAMA,
The *Ring* as drama, 5;
Wagner's ideas on, 1-2

DRAUPNIR,
A dwarf, 104;
Drops eight gold rings,
47, 104;
Froh gives to Gerd, 105;

DRAUPNIR *(Cont),*
Importance of name, 54;
Made by dwarfs, 104;
Placed on Balder's pyre,
104;
Wagner's ideas on rings,
111-112;
Wotan swears oath, 105;
Wotan's gold ring,
33, 104, 108

DRINK,
See: POTIONS

DROPPER,
Wotan's gold ring,
See: DRAUPNIR

DUTCH,
Teutonic peoples, 114, 117

DWARF,
Alberich, 42, 46, 51, 65, 98,
108, 109;
Andvari, 43, 105, 106, 108;
Brokk and Eitri, 104;
Draupnir, 104;
Metalsmiths, 32, 55, 108;
Ivaldi, 55

E

EAGLE,
A transformed giant, 65;
Hraesvelg creates the wind,
138;
Ill-omen, 13;
In World Ash Tree, 16, 138;
To feed the eagles, 86;
Wotan transforms himself
into, 45

EAST,
In *Ring*, 4

EASTERN BRANCH,
First manuscripts, 121;
Teutonic peoples, 117

EDDA,
See:
EDDA SAEMUNDAR
(*The Poetic Edda*)
THE PROSE EDDA

EDDA SAEMUNDAR
(*The Poetic Edda*),
Primary source for the *Ring* ,
126, 128;
Repository of Teutonic
myths, 127-128

EIKDYRNIR,
A hart, 16;
Munches leaves of Ljeradr,
20, 74

EINHERJAR,
See: CHAMPIONS

EITRI,
A dwarf, 32;
Forges Donner's
hammer, 33, 104;
Forges Froh's boar,
32-33, 104;
Forges Wotan's ring,
33, 104-105

ELDER EDDA, THE,
See: EDDA SAEMUNDAR

ELDHRIMNIR,
Kettle in Valhalla,
54, 75

ELM (Tree),
First mortal woman, 8, 11;
Synonym of mankind, 11

ELVES, LAND OF,
See: ALFHEIM

EMBLA,
First mortal woman, 8, 11

ENGLISH,
Teutonic peoples, 114

ERDE,
Mother of the Norns, 57

ETZEL,
German name of Attila (q.v.)

EURASIA,
Part of European Russia,
116, 117

EVIL-DOER, THE,
One of wotan's names, 45

EYLIMI,
King and father of Svava,
102-103

F

FADIR MORNA,
Father of swords, 86

FAFNER,
Aegishjalmr, 47-48;
Brother to Regin,
87, 91, 105;
Builds Valhalla, 67, 78;
Dragon, 13, 42, 43, 91, 106;
Guards a treasure, 88;
In *Ring*, 38-39;
Nibelung treasure 51;
Pact with Wotan, 60-61, 68;
Slays Fasolt, 23;
Slays his father, 91, 106, 108;
Slays Regin, 108;
Takes Freia, 64

FALCON,
Loge transforms himself into,
44

FALCON COAT,
Freia's coat
of transformation, 44, 47

FARMER,
Origin of farmers of the
world, 103

FAROESE,
Teutonic peoples, 114

FASOLT,
Builds Valhalla, 67, 78;
In *Ring*, 38-39;
Pact with Wotan, 60-61, 68;
Slain by Fafner, 23;
Takes Freia, 64

FATE,
See: CORD OF DESTINY

FATHER OF SWORDS,
Volund, 86

FEARFUL,
A river in Land of Giants,
136

FENRIR,
A wolf, Wotan's
killer, 54, 138;
In The Final Battle, 137;
Slain by Vidar, 86, 138;
Son of Loge, 137

FENSALIR,
Location of Fricka's home,
78

FERTILITY,
Froh, god of, 28;
The oak tree, 11

FIELD OF BATTLE,
Site of The Final
Battle, 75, 138

FIELD OF THE FOLK,
Location of Freia's home, 78

FINCH,
In *Ring*, 4

FIR (Tree),
In Germanic culture, 10-11;
In *Ring*, 4;
Stage setting in *Ring*, 11

FIRE,
One material of Rainbow
Bridge, 24;

FIRE *(Cont)*,
On mountain top, 57;
Wotan's spear, 57

FIRE-GIANTS,
See: GIANTS (Fire)

FJALAR,
To awaken giants at
ragnarök, 87, 136

FLAME OF WOUNDS,
A sword, 86

FLEMING,
Teutonic peoples, 114

FOE OF LOGE,
Heimdall, 26

FOLKVANGAR,
Location of Freia's home, 78

FOOD,
Kinds mentioned in
The Poetic Edda, 63;
Salmon, 106;
Wine, 63, 76

FOREST,
A culture, 7;
As boundaries, 9;
Setting for *Ring*, 11

FOREST BIRD,
In *Siegfried*, 12

FORGETFULNESS,
A potion, 11

FRANANG,
A waterfall, 43

FREIA,
A second name, 4;
Daughter of Njord, 134;
Giant wants her as wife, 32;
Gives apple (fertility) to
Rerir's wife, 68;
Goddess of the Golden
Apples, 69;

FREIA *(Cont)*,
  Goddess of Youth and
    Love, 64;
  Guardian of the Golden
    Apples, Chapter VII,
    63-70;
  Her attributes, 67;
  Her falcon-coat, 44;
  Her home, 78;
  In *Ring*, 38, 39;
  One of five gods in *Ring*, 66;
  One of her lovers, 87;
  Payment to giants, 67, 78-79;
  Ransomed from giants, 108;
  Relationship in *Ring*,
    134-135;
  Seeks information
    from wise-woman, 92;
  Sister of Froh, 134;
  Substitute for Idun, 27;
  Visits Valhalla, 78;
  Wagner makes Freia
    Guardian of the
    apples, 66, 68

FREKI,
  One of Wotan's two wolfs,
    76

FRICKA,
  Location of her home, 78;
  Mother of Balder and
    Hod, 75, 104;
  One of five gods in *Ring*, 66;
  Relationship in *Ring*,
    134-135;
  Wife of Wotan, 23, 75

FRISIAN,
  Western Branch of
    Teutonic peoples, 117

FROH,
  As compared with
    Heimdall, 26-27;
  Brother of Freia, 134;
  Causes Rainbow Bridge to
    appear, 23;
  Foremost god in Sweden, 27;
  Gives Draupnir to Gerd,
    105;

FROH *(Cont)*,
  God of Fertility, 28;
  God of the Fields, 28;
  His boar 32, 104;
  His magic sword, 47, 87;
  His runic mark, 28, 139;
  His ship, 32;
  Killed by Surt in
    The Final Battle, 138;
  Made Guardian of Rainbow
    Bridge, 27-28, 78;
  Member of Triad,
    27, 120-121;
  One of five gods in *Ring*, 66;
  Receives Svipdag's
    sword, 87;
  Relationship in *Ring*,
    134-135;
  Son of Njord, 134;
  Woos Gerd, 69

FROST-GIANTS,
  See: GIANTS (Frost)

G

GALATYR,
  A name for Wotan, 9

GANGLERI,
  A name for Wotan,
    50

GARM,
  Guard dog at gates of Hel,
    136

GATE OF THE SLAIN,
  Entry to Valhalla, 74

GATE SHELF,
  Wotan's primary seat, 78

GDANSK (Poland),
  Teutonic boundary, 115

GERD,
 A giantess, wooed by
  Froh, 69;
 Receives Froh's gift of
  Draupnir, 105

GERI,
 One of Wotan's two wolfs,
  76

GERMAN,
 Origin of the word, 114;
 Teutonic peoples, 114, 117

GERMANIA,
 A book by Tacitus, 114

GERMANIC,
 See: TEUTONIC

GERMANY,
 Origin of the word, 114

GIANT,
 Blain, 86;
 Brimir, 86;
 Build Valhalla, 23, 67, 78;
 How awakened at
  ragnarök, 87;
 Hrungnir, 34;
 Hrym, 137;
 Pact with Aesir gods, 79-80;
 Pact with Wotan, 60-61, 68;
 Skrymir, 34;
 Their world, 138;
 Thjasse, 31, 87;
 Transformed into eagle, 65;
 Will attack gods in
  The Final Battle, 80;
 See also:
  FAFNER
  FASOLT
  GIANT (Fire)
  GIANT (Frost)

GIANT (Fire),
 Cross Rainbow Bridge, 87;
 In The Final Battle, 137;
 Invade home of gods, 36;
 Surt, 24-25;
 Their home, 24, 138

GIANT (Frost),
 Steals Donner's hammer,
  34, 35;
 Their home, 17

GIBICHUNG,
 Child of Gibich, 98;
 Hall of, 22

GINNUNGAGAP,
 Yawning Gap, 17

GJALL,
 A drinking horn, 17

GJALLARHORN,
 A horn, 17;
 Heimdall's horn, 25;
 Sounded in
  The Final Battle, 137

GLADSHEIM,
 Location of Wotan's
  dwelling, 74

GLOVE,
 Iron gloves possessed by
  Donner, 31

GNITAHEITH,
 Fafner's lair, 106

GOAT,
 Donner's pair, 36;
 Heidrun, 74;
 In Ring, 8;
 In World Ash Tree, 16

GODDESS OF YOUTH
AND LOVE,
 Freia, 64

GODDESSES,
 See:
  FREIA
  FRICKA
  HEL
  IDUN
  IORD
  SIF

GOD OF POETRY,
Bragi, 66, 103

GOD OF THE FIELDS,
Froh, 28

GOD OF THE GALLOWS,
Wotan, 9

GOD OF THE HANGED,
Wotan, 9

GOD OF THE SWORD,
Tyr, 85

GOD OF WAR ,
Tyr, 85;
Wotan, 72

GODS,
At *ragnarök*, 136-137;
Await death in
Valhalla, 65-66;
German names in *Ring*, 121;
Helped by Loge, 66, 80;
Not immortal, 65;
Pact with a giant, 79;
Relationships, 134-135;
Their chef, 75;
The most venerated, 66;
See also:
BALDER
BRAGI
DONNER
FROH
HEIMDALL
HERMOD
HOD
HONIR
MAGNI
MODI
NJORD
TYR
ULL
VIDAR
WOTAN

GOLD,
A gold ring, 33, 47, 104;
Andvari's, 105;
Bryny, 48;
Eleven apples of gold, 69;
Froh's boar, 104;
"Golden" apples, 69;
Of the Rhine, 79;
Sif's hair, 32, 55;
Stolen from Rhinemaidens,
51;
Tarnhelm, 51;
The gods' ransom, 106;
Wotan's gift, 92;
See also:
TREASURE

GOLD BRISTLE,
Froh's boar, 32

GOLDEN APPLES,
See: APPLE

GOLD-TOOTHED,
Heimdall, 26

GOLD-TUFT,
Heimdall's horse, 25

GOLLINKAMBI,
A rooster, to awaken gods
at *ragnarök*, 136

GÖTTERDÄMMERUNG,
Conflicting stage directions,
57-58;
Freia's Golden Apples,
64-65;
Norn scene, 57;
Order of composition, 58;
Prelude, 22;
Ragnarök, 137;
Sacrifice of animals, 8;
Sieqfrieds Tod, 22;
Transformations, 42;
Valhalla, 77;
World Ash Tree, 19;
Wotan and Siegfried, 57

GRAM,
Cleaves an anvil, 89;
How Wagner used,
91-92, 95-96;
Its sharpness, 89;
Length, 91;
Linguistic history, 89;
Shattered, 90-91;
Siegfried's sword in Eddic
literature, 88-91;
Siegmund names, 91;
Thrust into tree, 89;
See also:
BALMUNG
NOTUNG
SWORD

GRANE,
Siegfried's horse, 80

GREEDY, THE,
One of Wotan's two wolfs,
76

GREY BEARD,
Wotan, 34-35

GRIMHILD,
Gunther's mother, 44;
Gunther's sister, 46;
Kills Hagen, 95;
Siegfried's treasure stolen
from her, 110;
Siegfried's wife, 94

GRIMM, JAKOB,
Deutsche Mythologie, 131

GRIMM, WILHELM,
Die deutsche Heldensage, 131

GUARDIAN OF VICTORY,
Siegmund, 97

GULLINBURSTI,
Froh's boar, 32

GULLINTANNI,
A name for Heimdall, 26

GULLTOPP,
Heimdall's horse, 25

GUNGNIR,
A weapon, 55, 56;
Grants victory, 47, 54;
Importance of name, 54;
In first war, 54, 134;
Its magic, 55;
Origin, 54-55;
Runes engraved on,
24, 59-61;
Wotan's spear, 18, 54, 56;
See also:
SPEAR (General)
SPEAR (*Ring*)

GUNNAR,
See: GUNTHER

GUNTHER,
A Gibichung, 98;
Brother to Grimhild, 46;
Brother to Gutrune, 98;
Gets Andvari's treasure, 107;
Involved in Siegfried's
death, 93;
King of Burgundy, 46;
Received message on a ring,
104;
Son of Grimhild, 44

GUTHRUN,
See: GUTRUNE

GUTRUN,
See: GUTRUNE

GUTRUNE,
A Gibichung, 98;
Gets Andvaranaut, 107;
Gives her treasure to
warriors, 103;
Gunther's sister, 98;
Sends message to Gunther,
104;
Weds Attila, 107;
Weds Siegfried, 107

H

HAFT DER WELT,
  Wotan's spear, 54

HAFT OF LORDSHIP,
  Wotan's spear, 54

HAFT OF POWER,
  Wotan's spear, 54

HAFT OF THE UNIVERSE,
  Wotan's spear, 54

HAGEN,
  Amazed at Siegfried's speed,
    42;
  Defeated in fight with
    Dietrich, 94;
  Gets Andvari's treasure, 107;
  Gets message on a ring, 104;
  Involved in Siegfried's
    death, 93;
  Killed by Grimhild, 95;
  Sinks Nibelung treasure in
    Rhine, 95, 110;
  Takes Balmung, 93;
  Urge to rule the world, 109

HAIR (Gold),
  Fashioned by dwarfs, 32, 55

HALFDAN,
  Donner's son, 31

HALLINSKIDI,
  Heimdall, 26

HALL OF THE CHOSEN,
  See: VALHALLA

HALL OF THE CHOSEN SLAIN,
  See: VALHALLA

HALL OF THE SLAIN,
  See: VALHALLA

HAMMER,
  A weapon of war, 83;
  See: MJOLLNIR

HANGATYR,
  Wotan, 9

HARBARD,
  Wotan, 34-35

HART,
  Eat World Ash Tree, 20, 74;
  Eikdyrnir, 16;
  Four in World Ash Tree, 16

HATI,
  A wolf in *ragnarök*, 136;
  Offspring of Fenrir, 137

HAWK,
  Vedrfolnir, 16

HAZEL (Tree),
  In *The Poetic Edda*, 11

HEAD,
  Heimdall's sword, 25

HEERFATHER,
  See: WOTAN

HEERSCHAFT HAFT,
  Wotan's spear, 54

HEGELING,
  See: SINTOLT,
        THE HEGELING

HEIDRUN,
  Gives mead for warriors in
    Valhalla, 74

HEIMDALL,
  As Rig, 103;
  Born of nine women, 25;
  Compared with Wotan,
    Donner, and Froh, 26-27;
  God of the Rainbow Bridge,
    25-27, 78, 103;
  His other names, 26;
  His sword, 25;

HEIMDALL (*Cont*),
Location of his home, 78;
Slain by Loge, 26;
Slays Loge, 138;
Sounds alarm at The Final
Battle, 137

HEIMSKRINGLA,
Source for the *Ring*,
126, 130-131

HEL (Mythical figure),
Called Hella, 4, 72;
Guardian of the Dead,
17, 105;
Her people will attack the
gods, 75, 137

HEL (Mythical place),
Bedecked with rings,
103-104;
Guard dog, 136;
Land of Dead, 72

HELGI,
A hero-warrior, 102;
Seeks to win Svava with
rings, 102-103

HELLA,
Guardian of the Dead, 4, 72;
See also: HEL

HELM OF DISGUISE,
See: TARNHELM

HELM OF TERROR,
Aegishjalmr, 47, 48

HERMOD,
Wotan's son, 105

HERO,
Dietrich, 88, 130;
Helgi, 102-103;
Svipdag, 31

HILL OF HEAVEN,
Heimdall's home, 78

HIMINBJORG,
Heimdall's home, 25, 78

HJORDIS,
Gives Siegfried pieces of his
father's sword, 91;
Mother of Siegfried, 91;
Siegmund's second wife, 90

HLIDSKJOLF,
Wotan's primary seat, 78

HOARD,
See: TREASURE

HOD,
Balder's brother and slayer,
75;
Raised in new world, 75;
Son of Wotan, 75

HOGNI,
See: HAGEN

HOLDA,
Ring name for Freia, 4

HOME,
Of each of the gods, 25, 78

HOME OF THE GODS,
See:
ASGARD
VALHALLA

HONEY,
Food in *The Poetic Edda*, 63

HONIR,
A god, 105;
A hostage in The First War,
134

HORN,
See:
GJALL
GJALLARHORN

HORSE,
A gift to Loge, 103;
Grane, 80;
Heimdall's, 25;
Helps build gods' stronghold,
67-68, 79;
In *Ring*, 4;
Loge transforms himself
into mare, 80;
Sign of battle, 12;
Sleipnir, 80;
Svadilfari, 79, 80

HOSTAGE,
In The First War, 134

HOVAMOL,
An Eddic poem, 18, 59

HRAESVELG,
An eagle, 138

HREIDMAR,
Demands ransom from
the gods, 106;
Father of Fafner, Otr,
and Regin, 43, 91;
Slain by Fafner, 91, 106, 108

HROTTI,
A sword, 88

HRUNGNIR,
A giant, 34

HRYM,
A giant, 137

HUGIN,
One of Wotan's ravens, 78

HUMAN,
'Purely human,' 2, 5, 126

HUNDING,
A king (Denmark), 90;
Challenge to Siegmund, 96;
Hunding's tree (Branstock),
14-15, 89;

HUNDING *(Cont)*,
Not qualified for
Valhalla, 81;
Slays Siegmund, 56, 81

HUN LAND (Hunland),
Attila's kingdom, 107

HVERGELMIR,
A spring, 16, 17;
Source of all rivers, 74

HYNDLA,
A wise-woman, 92

HYNDLULJOTH,
An Eddic poem, 92

I

ICELAND,
Northern religious thought,
120;
Teutonic region, 115;
Wotan's names there, 45;
See also: ICELANDER

ICELANDER,
Teutonic peoples, 114, 117;
See also: ICELAND

IDUN,
Bragi, her husband, 66, 103;
Guardian of the Apples,
27, 43, 66;
Magic of her apples, 68;
Rescued by Loge, 44;
Transformed into a nut, 43

IORD,
Donner's mother, 134;
Goddess of the Earth, 8

IRING,
A Danish prince, 88

IRMING,
See:
WITTIG, THE IRMING

IVALDI,
A dwarf metalsmith, 55

IVALDI'S SONS,
Forged Wotan's spear, 54-55

J

JORMUNGANDER,
See: MIDGARDSORM

JOTUNHEIM,
Land of the Giants, 138

K

KARL,
Son of Rig, 103

KEEN BITER,
A sword, 86

KING,
Hunding (Denmark), 90;
Nibelung, 93;
Nidud, 102;
Rig (Heimdall), 26

KING HUNDING,
Father of Lyngi, 90

KING OF THE GODS,
See: WOTAN

KLAGE, DIE,
Addition to *Nibelungenlied*,
129

L

LACHMANN, KARL,
Scholar of Teutonic myths,
126, 130-131

LAEVATEIN,
Loge's sword, 87

LAND OF THE DARK ELVES,
Svartalfheim, 138

LAND OF THE DEAD,
Niflheim, 138

LAND OF THE ELVES,
Alfheim, 138

LAND OF THE FIRE GIANTS,
Muspellsheim, 24, 138

LAND OF THE GIANTS,
Jotunheim, 138

LAND OF THE GODS (Aesir),
Asgard (q.v.)

LAND OF THE GODS (Vanir),
Vanaheim, 138

LAY OF THRYM, THE,
An Eddic poem, 34

LAYS OF THE GODS,
Edda Saemundar, 127

LAYS OF THE HEROES,
Edda Saemundar, 127-128

LIGHTNING,
Mjollnir, Donner's hammer,
35, 37

LINDEN (Tree),
In myth, 12;
In *Ring*, 4

LJERADR,
A tree, 16;
Grows near Valhalla, 74

LOGE,
Aids Donner, 34;
Aids gods, 68, 80;
At *ragnarök*, 136-137;
Cuts Sif's hair, 54;
Donner's hammer, 32;
Father of Fenrir, 137;
Father of Sleipnir, 80;
Fire will consume universe,
57;
Has inspected Valhalla, 77;
His sword, 87;
In Nibelheim, 42;
In The Final Battle, 137;
Involved in Balder's death,
43;
Promised gifts by Bragi, 103;
Relationship to gods,
134-135;
Rescues Idun, 44;
Slays Heimdall, 26, 138;
Slays Otr (Otter), 106;
Steals Andvari's treasure,
106, 108;
Threatened by Donner, 34;
To surround mountain top
with fire, 57;
Transformed into a mare,
43, 80;
Transformed into a salmon,
42;
Transforms Idun into a nut,
43;
Transforms into a falcon, 44;
Travels with Donner, 11;
Travels with Wotan,
105-106;
Will captain a ship at
ragnarök, 75

LOHENGRIN,
Critical piece by Franz
Mueller, 126

LORD OF THE RUNES,
Wotan, 140

LORD OF WARRIORS,
Wotan, 72

LOVE (Mortal),
Wagner's ideas on, 110-111

LOVER OF MURDER,
Mjollnir, 37

LYNGI,
Kills Siegmund, 91;
Slain by Siegfried, 91;
Son of King Hunding, 90;
Woos Hjordis, 90

M

MAGIC,
Alberich's ring, 51, 109;
Apples, 64-66;
Falcon-coat, 44;
Froh's sword, 47;
Gold ring (Draupnir), 47;
Hammer (Mjollnir), 34, 47;
Helm of Terror
(Aegishjalmr), 47, 48;
Iron gloves, 31;
Runes, 139-141;
Tarnhelm, 42, 51;
Tarnkappe, 45-46;
Wotan's spear (Gungnir),
47, 55;
See also: CHARMS

MAGNI,
Donner's son, 37

MAIL-COAT,
See: BRYNY

MAIN (River),
Teutonic boundary, 117

MARK (Mark),
Boundary, 9

MAULER,
Donner's hammer,
See: MJOLLNIR

MEAD,
 Drink in Valhalla, 16;
 Drink of Inspiration, 45;
 Food in *The Poetic Edda*, 63;
 From the goat Heidrun, 74

MEMORY,
 One of Wotan's two ravens,
 78

MIDDLE ENCLOSURE,
 Land of Mortals, 78;
 See also: MIDGARD

MIDGARD,
 Creation, 7-8;
 Land of Mortals, 78, 138;
 Where located, 17

MIDGARDSORM
(Popular name for Jormungander),
 At *ragnarök*, 136;
 In The Final Battle, 137-138;
 World Serpent, 34, 37

MIGHT,
 Donner's son, 37

MILKY WAY,
 Known as 'Wotan's Way,' 23

MIMAMEID,
 World Ash Tree, 17

MIME,
 Much like Regin, 108;
 Possesses Notung, 13;
 Tarnhelm, 42;
 Urge to rule the world, 109

MIMIR,
 A hostage in The First War,
 134;
 A water spirit, 17;
 At *ragnarök*, 136;
 Steals Thjasse's sword, 31, 87

MIMUNG,
 Dietrich's sword, 88
 Dietrich's teacher, 88

MISTLETOE,
 Grows near Valhalla, 75;
 Involved in Balder's death,
 75

MJOLLNIR,
 By whom made, 32-33, 104;
 Causes lightning and
 thunder, 35, 37;
 Clears sky of mists, 23;
 Donner's first hammer, 31;
 Donner's hammer,
 Chapter IV, 31-39;
 How made, 32-33;
 Importance of name, 54;
 Instrument of consecration
 and resurrection, 36;
 In The Final Battle, 36-37;
 Its use and powers,
 34, 36, 47;
 Loge's part in its origin, 32;
 Most celebrated of Teutonic
 ideas, 31;
 Represents the good, 37;
 Short of handle, 33, 87;
 Slays a giant, 80;
 Stolen by Thrym, 34;
 Swastica, 35;
 The Christian Cross, 37-38;
 The name, 31-32, 54;
 Threatens Fafner and
 Fasolt, 56;
 Wagner's ideas about, 38-39

MODI,
 Donner's son, 37

MONE, FRANZ JOSEF,
 Scholar of Teutonic myths,
 126, 130-131

MOON,
 Payment to giants, 67-68, 79

MOUNT OF HEAVEN,
 Heimdall's home, 25

MUELLER, FRANZ,
  Correspondent with
    Wagner, 126-127

MUNIN,
  One of Wotan's ravens, 78

MURDER,
  Serious crime, 80

MUSPELLSHEIM,
  Land of Fire, 24;
  One of the nine worlds of
    the universe, 138

MYTH,
  Edda Saemundar, 127-128;
  Examples in Ring, 4;
  Origin of Teutonic myths,
    116, 118, 120;
  Volsungasaga, 128-129;
  Wagner and Donner's
    hammer, 38-39;
  Wagner and golden apples,
    66, 69-70;
  Wagner and Rainbow
    Bridge, 29;
  Wagner and rings, 107-112;
  Wagner and swords,
    91-92, 95-96;
  Wagner and Tarnhelm, 52;
  Wagner and World Ash
    Tree, 21;
  Wagner and Wotan's spear,
    61;
  Wagner and Valhalla,
    77, 81-82;
  Wagner's concepts, 2;
  Wagner's knowledge of,
    5, 125-128, 131;
  Wagner's use of, 122-123

N

NAMES,
  Importance of, 54, 87;
  On swords, 87-88;
  See also:
    ANDVARANAUT
    BALMUNG

NAMES (Cont),
  GRAM
  GUNGNIR
  MJOLLNIR
  NOTUNG
  VALHALLA
  YGGDRASIL

NANNA,
  Balder's wife, 36

NIBELHEIM,
  Home of the Nibelung
    dwarfs (Ring), 42

NIBELUNG,
  Alberich, 98;
  Child of fog, 98;
  King Nibelung, 93;
  Son of King Nibelung, 93;
  Treasure, 51, 64-65;
  Wagner's name for race of
    dwarfs, 42

NIBELUNGENLIED,
  Primary source for the Ring,
    126;
  Source of 'German essence,'
    129-130

NIBELUNGEN NOT UND
DIE KLAGE,
  SEE: NIBELUNGENLIED

NIDAVELLIR,
  World of the Dwarfs, 138

NIDHOGG,
  A serpent, 16, 17;
  Gnaws on World Ash Tree,
    20

NIDUD,
  A king, 102

NIFLHEIM,
  Land of the Dead, 17, 138

NINE,
Charmed number, 18;
Heimdall son of nine
women, 25;
Loge's sword secured by
nine locks, 87;
Nine worlds, 10, 16,
24, 50, 87;
The nine worlds of the
universe, 138;
Wotan hangs from World
Ash tree for
nine nights, 59

NJORD,
Father of Froh and Freia,
134

NORNIR,
See: NORNS

NORNS,
Daughters of Erde, 57;
Fated Andvari to a
waterfall, 105;
Indicate Wotan will set
world ablaze, 58;
Meet at base of
World Ash tree,
19, 22, 55;
Norn scene, when written,
58;
Talk of Wotan's shattered
spear, 57;
The three Norns, 17;
Wagner's Norns, 20

NORSE (Old),
Mother tongue, 119

NORTH,
In Ring, 4

NORTHERN BRANCH,
Originators of Teutonic
mythology, 122;
Teutonic peoples, 117;
Wagner's use of writings,
122, 128-129

NORWAY,
Part of northern religious
thought, 120;
Teutonic region, 115;
Wotan in, 45;
See also: NORWEGIAN

NORWEGIAN,
Teutonic peoples, 114, 117;
See also: NORWAY

NOTUNG,
Broken on Wotan's spear,
57;
Chapter IX, 83-99;
Fades with Siegfried's death,
98;
Forged by Regin, 89;
In Hunding's tree, 14, 97;
Linguistic history 97-98;
Reforged by Siegfried, 13-14;
Rune, 139;
Siegmund withdraws sword,
97;
Siegmund's, 53, 88;
See also:
BALMUNG
GRAM
SWORD

NUT,
Food in The Poetic Edda, 63;
Idun transformed into, 43

O

OAK (Tree),
Associated with Donner,
11, 15;
Drink of Forgetfulness, 11;
Grows near Valhalla, 75;
Hunding's tree (Branstock),
14-15;
Its cures, 11;
Siegfried's pyre, 11;
Wotan thrusts sword into, 89

OAK-THORNED, THE,
A hart, 16, 74

OATH,
Seriousness of a broken
oath, 80, 105;
Sworn on a spear, 103;
Sworn on a sword, 84, 103;
Wotan swears oath on a
ring, 105

ODER (River),
Teutonic boundary, 117

ODIN,
Wotan, 121

OTHAN,
Wotan, 121

OTHIN,
Wotan, 121

OTHUR,
Wotan, 121

OTR,
Becomes an otter, 105-106;
Son of Hreidmar, 43

OTTER,
See: OTR

OXEN,
In *Ring*, 8

P

PACT,
Gods' pact with a giant,
67-68, 79;
Runes on Wotan's spear, 60;
Wotan's pact with giants, 67

PIG,
Used to forge Froh's boar,
32

PINE (Tree),
Setting (Tannewald)
in *Ring*, 11-12

PLEDGE,
On a sword, 84;
Runes on Wotan's spear, 60;
Wotan's pledge to giants, 64

POEM OF HYNDLA, THE,
An Eddic poem, 92

POETIC EDDA, THE,
See: EDDA SAEMUNDAR

POLAND,
Teutonic boundary, 115

POTION,
Drink of Forgetfulness, 11;
Magic drink, 10

PROSE EDDA, THE,
Ragnarök, 54

PROTO INDO-EUROPEAN,
First language of Teutonic
peoples, 116

PUNISHMENT,
Broken oath and murder, 80;
Capital, 8-9

PURELY HUMAN,
In drama, 2, 5, 126

PYRE,
Ring placed on Balder's
pyre, 104;
Siegfried's 11, 21, 57;
When set afire, 58

Q

QUIVERING PATHWAY,
Rainbow Bridge, 24

QUIVERING ROADWAY,
Rainbow Bridge, 24

R

RAGNARÖK,
Cause, 105;
Cock will awaken giants, 87;
Cock will awaken gods, 136;
Depiction, 135-137;
End of world, 36, 64,
135-137;
Linguistic history, 135;
Valhalla survives, 74;
Volva predicts, 75;
World Ash Tree, 16, 21;
Wotan at, 54

RAINBOW BRIDGE, THE,
Bifrost, 18, 23-24;
Bilrost, 23-24;
Bridge of the Aesir Gods,
24;
Chapter III, 23-29;
Dramatic property in *Ring*,
29;
Entrance to Valhalla, 23;
Fire-Giants, 24, 36, 87;
Froh (Guardian), 27-28;
Heimdall, 25-27, 103;
Regenbogenbrücke, 23, 77;
Runes engraved, 24;
Surt will cross, 24-26;
The Final Battle, 24, 137

RAM,
Heimdall, 26

RATATOSK,
A squirrel, 16

RAVEN,
Good luck sign, 86;
War, 86;
Wotan's, 21, 78

RAVENOUS, THE,
One of Wotan's two wolves,
76

RED,
One color of Rainbow
Bridge, 24

REDIL,
Also called *Refil*, 88;
Regin's sword, 87

REFIL,
Also called *Redil*, 87;
Regin's sword, 88

REGENBOGENBRÜCKE,
Rainbow Bridge, 23

REGIN,
Brother to Otr, 105;
Fafner's mythical brother,
87, 91;
Forges sword Gram, 89, 91;
Foster father to Siegfried,
87-88, 91;
His sword, 87, 88

RELIGION,
Early Teutonic, 118, 120;
Runes, 139-141;
Two bodies of thought, 120

RERIR,
Grandson of Wotan, 68

RESURRECTION,
Balder, 36

RHEINGOLD, DAS,
Donner's hammer, 38;
Freia's golden apples, 64;
Rainbow Bridge, 23, 29, 77;
Transformations, 42;
Valhalla, 39, 77;
Wotan's spear, 56

RHINE,
Mythical source, 74;
Nibelung treasure in its
waters, 95, 110;
Nibelung treasure travels
the Rhine, 109;
Teutonic boundary, 115, 117

RHINE DAUGHTERS,
See: RHINEMAIDENS

RHINEMAIDENS,
Gold (Tarnhelm), 41, 51;
Waltraute pleads on their
behalf, 65

RICH IN SEATS,
Freia's home, 78

RIG,
Heimdall, 26, 103

RIGHTS,
First son, 93

RIN,
Nordic name for *Rhine*, 74

RING (Jewelry),
Acquired by force, 108;
A gift to Loge, 103;
A gift to *volva*, 103;
Alberich makes, 51, 108;
Andvaranaut (Andvari's
ring), 105-107;
As treasure, 102, 108;
Carried messages, 104, 107;
Chapter X, 101-112;
Cultural uses, 101-102;
Draupnir (Wotan's), 33, 104;
Force to rule the world,
109-110, 111;
Gift from Froh, 105;
In Brünnhilde's possession,
65;
In Hel, 103-104;
In *Ring*, 108-112;
Its end (Drama), 52;
Part of Gutrune's treasure,
103;
Predicts Attila's death, 104;
Prized as gifts, 102-103;
Ring placed on Balder's
pyre, 104, 105;
Rings for Karl and Snora,
103;
Siegfried gives ring to
Brünnhilde, 103, 107, 108;
Sign of welcome, 103;

RING (Jewelry) *(Cont),*
Stimulus for the *Ring*, 102;
Symbol of marriage, 103;
Volund has 700, 102;
Wagner's ideas on rings,
111-112

RING DES NIBELUNGEN, DER,
As mythology, 2-3;
Blend of two worlds,
125-126;
Dates of composition,
1, 42, 125;
Dramatic intent, 4;
Edda Saemundar, 127-128;
Fifty copies published by
Wagner, 126;
German names, 121;
Major theme, 112;
Nibelungenlied, 129-130;
Order of composition, 58;
Original sketch, 125;
Premiere, 5;
Secondary sources, 130-131;
Sources, 126;
Volsungasaga, 128-129;
Wilkinasaga, 130

RING OF THE NIBELUNG, THE,
See: DER RING DES
NIBELUNGEN

ROARING,
A river, 74

ROARING CAULDRON,
A spring (Hvergelmir),
16, 74

ROOSTER,
See: FJALAR
GOLLINKAMBI

ROSE (Tree),
In *The Poetic Edda*, 11

ROWAN (Tree),
In *The Poetic Edda*, 11

RUNE,
Basic data, 139-141;
Carved on wood, 59;
Carved on World Ash Tree,
19, 24;
Carved on Wotan's spear,
20, 59, 60;
Froh's rune, 139;
Froh's runic mark, 28;
Loge uses runes to
make a sword, 87;
Naud (Not), 97;
Runes of fate, 17;
Runic inscriptions, 121;
Tree (branch) runes, 9-10;
Tyr's runic mark, 85;
Union of Wotan and runes,
59;
Wotan takes up, 18, 59

RUSSIA,
Dispersion of its early
people, 116

S

SACRIFICE,
Animal, 8

SAEHRIMNIR,
Boar eaten in Valhalla, 75

SAGA OF THE VOLSUNGS,
See: VOLSUNGASAGA

SALMON,
As food, 106;
Loge transforms himself
into, 43;

SCANDINAVIA,
Vikings, 72, 83, 122

SCHILBUNG,
Son of King Nibelung, 93

SEA HALLS, THE,
Location of Fricka's
home, 78

SEEKER OF
FREIA'S NECKLACE,
Heimdall, 26

SERPENT,
Alberich becomes, 42;
Blood Snake, 86;
Jormungander, 34;
Nidhogg, 16, 17, 20;
Regin's sword, 88;
See also:
WORLD SERPENT

SESSRUMNIR,
Freia's home, 78

SHEEP,
In Ring, 8

SHELF OF THE SLAIN,
Wotan's home, 78

SHE-WOLF,
Eats Volsung's sons, 90;
See also: WOLF

SHRIEKING HORN,
Sound heard around the
world, 25;
Sounded in The Final Battle,
137

SIEGFRIED,
Born, 91;
First rights, 93;
Gains a gold bryny, 48;
Gains Helm of Terror, 48;
Gains Tarnkappe, 46, 48;
Gets Andvaranaut, 106;
Gives Brünnhilde a ring,
103;
Grandson of Volsung, 68, 98;
Hagen takes Balmung, 93;
His death, 93, 107;
His foster father,
87-88, 89, 91;
His pyre, 11, 21, 57, 58;
His sword, 88;
Overcomes Brünnhilde,
46, 107;

SIEGFRIED *(Cont)*,
Presents Andvaranaut to
Gerd, 107;
Receives Balmung, 93;
Shatters Wotan's spear, 57;
Siegfried legend, 125, 128;
Slays Lyngi, 91;
The awakener, 10;
To divide King Nibelung's
treasure, 93;
To learn fear, 13;
Uses Tarnhelm, 42, 43-44

SIEGFRIED (Music-drama),
Ash tree, 13;
Brünnhilde's wisdom, 10;
Linden tree, 12;
The sword, 92;
Wotan and Siegfried meet,
57

SIEGLINDE,
A Volsung twin, 50;
Cannot enter Valhalla, 81;
Mother of Siegfried, 81

SIEGMUND,
A Volsung twin, 50;
Brother to Signy, 89;
Challenge from Hunding, 96;
Decreed to die, 80;
Father of Sinfjotli, 90;
Freed from captivity, 90;
Killed by Lygni, 90;
Marries Borghild, 90;
Marries Hjordis, 90;
Notung, 96-97;
Slain by Hunding, 56, 81;
Son of Volsung, 68;
Withdraws Gram from tree,
89, 97;
Wotan gives sword, 92

SIF,
Donner's wife, 32;
Hair fashioned by Ivaldi, 54;
Has hair of gold, 32

SIGGEIR,
Cannot withdraw sword
from tree, 90;
Dies in fire set by
Siegmund, 90;
Husband to Signy, 89

SIGNY,
Aids Siegmund, 90;
Dies in fire set by
Siegmund, 90;
Mother of Sinfjotli, 90;
Sister to Siegmund, 89

SIGRDRIFA,
Brünnhilde, 10

SIGRLIN,
Daughter of a king, 102

SINFJOTLI,
Murdered by Borghild, 90;
Son of Siegmund and his
sister, Signy, 90

SINTOLT, THE HEGELING,
A *Ring* hero, 80

SKIDBLADNIR,
Fashioned by Ivaldi, 54;
Froh's ship, 32

SKIRNIR,
Froh's servant, 69

SKOLL,
A wolf at *ragnarök*, 136;
Offspring of Fenrir, 137

SKRYMIR,
A giant, 34

SKULL,
A Norn, 17

SKY GOD,
Wotan, 72

SLEEP,
Brünnhilde's banishment,
56-57

SLEIPNIR,
Wotan's stallion,
son of Loge, 80

SLEITH,
A river in Land of the
Giants, 136

SMITH (Metal),
Donner's hammer, 33, 104;
Froh's boar, 32-33, 104;
Froh's ship, 32, 55;
Froh's sword, 87;
Sif's gold hair, 32, 55;
Wotan's ring,
33, 104-105, 108;
Wotan's spear, 32, 54-55

SNOR,
Wife of Karl, 103

SONG OF RIG,
An Eddic poem, 103

SONG OF THE NIBELUNGS,
See: NIBELUNGENLIED

SOOTY-FACED,
Chef to the gods, 75

SOOTY WITH FIRE,
Cooking kettle in Valhalla,
54, 75

SOUTH,
Excluded from *Ring*, 4

SOUTHERN GERMANIC
THOUGHT,
Region, 120;
Used in *Ring*, 121, 129-130

SPAN,
A measurement, 91;
See also: GRAM

SPEAR (General),
As a weapon, 83, 53-54, 134;
Guards sanctity of oath, 103;
See also:
GUNGNIR
SPEAR (*Ring*)

SPEAR (*Ring*),
At end of universe, 57;
Chapter VI, 53-61;
Incorporation into libretto,
55-56;
Origin, 20, 54-55, 59;
Reflects mythical
essence, 61;
Runes engraved on, 59-61;
Significance, 58-59;
Significant references to, 54;
Symbol of authority,
56-57, 59;
Wotan's, 53, 54;
Wotan thrusts spear into
Loge, 21, 57;
See also:
GUNGNIR
SPEAR (General)

SPELLS,
In drink, 10;
See also:
CHARMS
MAGIC

SPRING,
Hvergelmir, 16, 17;
Mimir's (Spring of Wisdom),
17, 20, 136;
Urd's, 17

SPRING OF WISDOM,
At *ragnarök*, 136;
Mimir's, 17, 20

SQUIRREL,
Ratatosk, 16

STEED OF YGG,
Wotan, 15

STRONG,
Donner's home, 78

STURLUSON, SNORRI,
Heimskringla, 131;
The Prose Edda, 79

SUN,
Payment to giants, 67-68, 79

SUPREME GOD,
Wotan, 23, 49, 60, 120

SURT,
Crosses Rainbow Bridge, 87;
His sword, 87;
In The Final Battle, 137;
Kills Froh at *ragnarök*, 138;
Leader of Fire-Giants,
24-25

SVADILFARI,
A giant's stallion, 79, 80

SVARTALFAHEIM,
Land of the Dark Elves, 138

SVAVA,
Wooed by Helgi, 102-103

SVIPAL,
Wotan, 45

SVIPDAG,
A hero, 31;
Cleaves Donner's hammer,
87;
One of Freia's lovers, 87

SWAN,
In Urd's spring, 17-18

SWASTIKA,
Donner's hammer, 35

SWEDEN,
Froh, the foremost god, 27;
Part of northern religious
thought, 120;
Teutonic region, 115;
See also: SWEDISH

SWEDISH,
Teutonic peoples, 114, 117;
See also: SWEDEN

SWIFT MOVING,
Regin's sword, 87

SWIFT TUSKED, THE,
A squirrel, 16

SWORD,
As wealth, 85;
A weapon, 83;
Brimir's, 86;
Cleaves Donner's hammer,
87;
Dietrich's, 88;
Eddic verses, 98-99;
Fafner's, 88;
Father of swords, 86;
Figurative language, 86;
Froh's, 44, 87;
Gift to Loge, 103;
Guards sanctity of oath,
103;
Heimdall's, 25;
How Wagner adapted,
91-92, 95-96;
Illumine Valhalla, 76;
Instrument of truth, 84;
Iring's, 88;
Its god, 84-85;
Loge's, 87;
Regin's, 87-88;
Significance in Germanic
culture, 83-85;
Signs for use of, 86;
Surt's, 87;
Sword of Victory, 87;
Thrust into tree, 89-90;
See also:
BALMUNG
GRAM
NOTUNG

SWORD OF VICTORY,
Forged by Thjasse,
a giant, 87

T

TACITUS,
Germania, 114

TANNEWALD,
Ring setting, 11

TARNHELM,
Aegishjalmr, 47-48;
Alberich's magic, 51;
Chapter V, 41-52;
Falcon-coat, 47;
Its end, 51-52;
Its gold, 51;
Tarnkappe, 45-46;
Transformation,
41, 42-45;
Wagner's creation,
41-42, 48-49, 51;
Wagner's skill at
adaptation, 52;
Wotan, 50

TARNKAPPE,
A magic cloak, 45-46;
First owned by Alberich, 46;
How used, 46;
Its end, 51

TEUTON (Teutones),
Active tribe, 114, 117

TEUTONDOM,
Related words, 115;
The Teutonic regions, 115ts

TEUTONIC,
Communal societies, 119;
Cultural development,
117-118;
Early religion, 118;
First language, 116;
First name of people, 114;
Languages, 114;
Nationalities, 114;
Origin of Teutonic peoples,
115-116;
Related words, 115;
The early culture, 113;
The word, 113, 114-115;
Three branches of peoples,
117

TEUTONISM,
See: TEUTONDOM

TEUTONIST,
See: TEUTONDOM

TEUTONIZE,
See: TEUTONDOM

THEODORIC,
See: DIETRICH

THIDREK,
See: DIETRICH

THIDREKSSAGA,
See: WILKINASAGA

THJASSE,
A giant, 31;
Forges Sword of Victory, 87;
Mimir steals sword, 87;
Thjasse and Volund, 87

THOR,
Donner's Nordic name, 35

THOUGHT,
One of Wotan's ravens, 78

THRUSTER,
A sword, 88

THRYM,
Steals Donner's hammer,
34, 35;
Wants Freia as wife, 34

THRYMSVIDA,
An Eddic poem, 34

THUND,
A river, 74

THUNDER,
Donner's hammer, 35, 37

TIME,
How counted, 18;
Wotan and nine nights, 59

TOAD,
In *Ring*, 4

TORUN (Poland),
Teutonic boundary, 115

TRANSFORMATION,
Andvari's, 105;
Fafner's,
42-43, 47, 91, 106;
Idun's, 43;
In Mythical literature, 44;
In North and South, 45;
In *Ring,* 41-43, 52;
Loge's, 43-44, 80;
Otr's, 43, 105-106;
Siegfried's, 43-44;
Wotan's, 44-45

TREASURE,
Alberich's, 51;
Andvari's, 105-107;
A sword, 84;
Helgi will possess, 102;
Hreidmar's, 91;
King Nibelung's, 93, 109;
Nibelung, 51, 64;
Representing beauty, 102;
Rings, 64-65, 102, 103;
Siegfried gains, 46, 48;
Sunk in the Rhine, 95, 110;
Volund's 700 rings, 102;
See also: GOLD

TREE,
Associated with worship, 7-8;
Hunding's, 14-15;
Ljeradr, 16;
Mimir's, 17;
Ring setting, 11-12;
Runes, 9-10;
Tannewald, 11-12;
Tree of battle, 9;
Tree of war, 13;
Used as boundaries, 9;
Used for capital
punishment, 8;
Wolf-tree, 8;
Yggdrasil, 15-21, 74, 138;
See also:
ASH
ASPEN
BEECH
BIRCH

TREE *(Cont),*
ELM
FIR
HAZEL
LINDEN
OAK
PINE
ROSE
ROWAN
WORLD ASH
YEW

TREMULOUS PATHWAY,
Rainbow Bridge, 24

TREMULOUS ROADWAY,
Rainbow Bridge, 24

TRIAD,
Wotan, Donner, Froh,
27, 120-121
TRUTH,
Basic, 2;
In *Ring,* 5;
Runes on Wotan's spear, 60;
Sword, 84

TUESDAY,
Tyr, 85

TURNER, THE,
Heimdall, 26

TYR,
God of the Sword, 85;
God of War, 85;
His rune, 85;
Linguistic variations, 85;
Tiw's Day, 85

U

ULL,
God of Archers, 11

UNG,
Child of, 98

URD,
  A Norn, 17;
  First Norn, 20;
  Her spring, 17

V

VALASKJOLF,
  Wotan's home, 78

VALFADER,
  Wotan, 76

VALGRIND,
  Entrance to Valhalla, 74

VALHALLA (Mythical),
  Abode of slain warriors,
    12-13, 16, 71, 72;
  Animals, 74;
  Balder's residence, 36;
  Built by the gods, 71, 78;
  Chapter VIII, 71-82;
  Compared with
    Donner's hammer, 31;
  Cooking kettle, 54;
  Description, 74-76;
  Food served, 54, 63;
  Germanic beliefs, 71-73;
  Linguistic history
    of names, 73;
  Location, 16;
  Survives *ragnarök*, 74;
  Wotan's army, 12, 20, 137;
  Wunschmädchen, 76;
  See also:
    VALHALLA (Ring)

VALHALLA (Ring),
  Built by giants,
    23, 67, 78-79;
  Chapter VIII, 71-82;
  First seen, 39;
  For males only, 81;
  Gods await their doom,
    65, 66;
  Gods enter for first time,
    23;

VALHALLA (Ring) (Cont),
  Home of the Gods,
    21, 64, 77;
  Loge inspected, 77;
  Wagner's adherence to
    myths, 81-82;
  Wagner's source for method
    of construction, 79-80;
  Waltraute leaves, 64-65;
  Wotan designed, 78;
  See also:
    VALHALLA (Ring)

VALKYRIE,
  Brünnhilde, 10, 22;
  Serve Wotan in Valhalla, 76;
  Transport slain warriors
    to Valhalla, 76;
  Wunschmädchen, 76

VALKYRIE ROCK,
  Brünnhilde sleeps, 57;
  Valkyries' gathering place,
    42

VANAHEIM,
  Land of the Vanir Gods, 138

VANIR,
  A race of gods, 24, 134;
  The First War, 54, 79;
  Their home, 138

VEDRFOLNIR,
  A hawk, 16

VEGTAM,
  Wotan, 50

VERDANDI,
  A Norn, 17

VIDAR,
  Avenges Wotan's death, 138;
  Son of Wotan, 86

VIGRID,
  Site of The Final Battle,
    75, 138

VIKING,
    Age of, 72, 83, 122

VILKINA SAGA,
    See: WILKINASAGA

VINDLER,
    Heimdall, 26

VISTULA,
    Teutonic boundary, 115, 117

VODAN,
    Wotan, 121

VODEN,
    Wotan, 121

VOLSUNG,
    Father of Siegmund, 68, 89;
    Father of Signy, 89;
    Is slain, 90;
    Most famous of the clan, 91;
    Siegfried, 13, 22;
    Son of Rerir, 68;
    Volsung's hall, 14, 89;
    Volsung twins, 50;
    Wälsung, 98

VOLSUNGASAGA,
    Nordic version of the
        Siegfried legend, 128-129;
    Primary source for the *Ring*,
        126, 128

VOLUND,
    A ring stolen from him,
        102, 108;
    Father of Swords, 86;
    Has 700 rings, 102;
    Volund and Thjasse, 87

VOLVA,
    A 'wise-woman,' 53-54;
    Predicts *ragnarök*, 75, 76;
    Tells Wotan of welcome
        prepared for Balder, 104;
    Wotan gives *volva* a ring, 103

VOSFUD,
    Wotan, 50

VOTHEN,
    Wotan, 121

VULNERABILITY,
    Siegfried's, 93

W

WALDVOGEL,
    See: FOREST BIRD

WALHALL,
    Valhalla, 73

WALKÜRE, DIE,
    Hunding's tree, 14;
    Siegmund-Brünnhilde, 81;
    The sword, 89, 92;
    Wotan's spear, 56

WÄLSE,
    Volsung, 98

WÄLSUNG,
    Child of Wälse, 98

WALTRAUTE,
    Leaves Valhalla, 64

WANDERER,
    Wotan, 50

WANES,
    A race of gods, 24, 134

WAR,
    A war culture, 83;
    To feed the eagles, 86;
    To feed the ravens, 86;
    See also:
        THE FIRST WAR

WAR, THE FIRST,
    Aesir versus Vanir,
        54, 79, 134;
    See also: WAR

WARRIORS,
    See: CHAMPIONS

WARSAW (Poland),
Teutonic boundary, 115

WASKE,
A sword, 88

WATCHMAN OF THE GODS,
Heimdall, 25

WEALTH,
The sword, 84;
See also:
GOLD
TREASURE

WEAPONS,
Of early Teutondom, 83

WEATHER-BLEACHED,
A hawk, 16

WEDA,
Wotan, 121

WELT-ESCHE,
See: WORLD ASH TREE

WEST,
In *Ring*, 4

WESTERN BRANCH,
First manuscripts, 121-122;
Teutonic peoples, 117

WHITE GOD, THE,
Heimdall, 26, 27

WILKINASAGA,
Primary source for the *Ring*,
126;
Resume, 130

WINE,
Food in *The Poetic Edda*, 63;
Wotan's sustenance, 76

WISHING-ROD,
Power to rule the world,
109-110

WISH-MAIDENS,
See: WUNSCHMÄDCHEN

WISLA,
See: VISTULA

WITCH-WIFE,
Signy, 90

WITTIG, THE IRMING,
A *Ring* hero, 80

WODAN,
Wotan, 121

WODEN,
Wotan, 121

WOLF,
Favorable sign for war, 13;
Fenrir, Wotan's killer,
54, 86, 137, 138;
In *Ring*, 4;
She-wolf, 90;
Siegmund and Sinfjotli, 90;
When a good luck sign, 86;
Wolf-skin, 90;
Wolf-tree, 8;
Wotan's two wolves, 76

WOLF-SKIN,
Siegmund and Sinfjotli, 90;
See also: WOLF

WOLF-TREE,
As gallows, 8;
See also: WOLF

WOODBIRD,
See: FOREST BIRD

WOODEN,
Wotan, 121

WOODEN-BLADED,
Froh's ship, 32, 54

WORLD ASH TREE,
  Animals, 16, 74;
  Chapter II, 17-22;
  Functions, 4;
  Holiest of trees, 15;
  Houses nine worlds, 138;
  In *ragnarök*, 136;
  Norns, 17, 19-20;
  Place of Council, 24, 34;
  Possibly Ljeradr, 74;
  Principal representative of
    Teutonic thought, 7;
  Principal Teutonic belief, 19;
  References to, 15-16;
  Three roots, 17;
  Tree of Life, 18;
  Tree of the Universe, 14, 15;
  Welt-Esche, 15, 19;
  Withers and dies, 20-21; 55;
  Wotan hangs from, 18, 59;
  Wotan tears away branch,
    20;
  Yggdrasil, 15-21, 74, 138

WORLD OF MEN,
  See: MIDGARD

WORLD OF THE DWARFS,
  See: NIDAVELLIR

WORLD SERPENT,
  See: MIDGARDSORM

WOTAN,
  Allfather, 18, 21, 26,
    49, 54, 56, 60, 115;
  Andvari's treasure, 105-108;
  As compared with Heimdall,
    26-27;
  A sky god, 72;
  Associated with ash tree,
    12, 15, 18-19;
  Assumes form of an eagle,
    45;
  Assumes mortal form, 49-50;
  At *ragnarök*,
    55, 57, 75, 135-136;
  Attacked at *ragnarök*, 75;
  Awaits death in Valhalla,
    65-66;
  Balder, his son, 36, 75, 104;

WOTAN *(Cont)*,
  Bedecks Hel with rings,
    103-104;
  Compared with Donner
    and Froh, 120;
  Designs Valhalla, 78;
  Father of Balder and Hod,
    75;
  Fenrir, his killer, 54, 86, 138;
  Fricka's husband, 23, 75;
  Gets runes, 59;
  Gives an eye, 17, 20, 136;
  Gives *volva* a ring, 103;
  God of the Gallows, 9;
  God of the Hanged, 9;
  God of War, 72;
  Grandfather of Rerir, 68;
  Grey Beard, 34-35;
  Hangs from World Ash
    Tree, 18, 59;
  Heerfather, 18, 92;
  His divine authority
    destroyed, 57;
  His dress, 50;
  His gift to the world, 92;
  His gold ring (Draupnir),
    32, 104-105;
  His home, 78;
  His primary seat, 78;
  His sacred hall, 71;
  His spear, Chapter VI,
    53-61;
  His stallion, 80;
  His two ravens, 78;
  His two wolfs, 76;
  In Iceland and Norway, 45;
  In Nibelheim, 42;
  In Northern and Southern
    thought, 120;
  Interposes spear as authority
    56;
  Invocation of, 9;
  King of the Gods, 34, 44,
    49, 55, 56, 57, 60, 61, 71,
    74, 76, 89, 104, 107;
  Location of his home, 74;
  Lord of Warriors, 72;
  Lord of the Runes, 140;
  Master of transformations,
    44-45, 49, 89;
  Meals in Valhalla, 75-76;

WOTAN (*Cont*),
  Meets Siegfried, 57;
  Member of Triad,
    27, 120-121;
  Milky Way, 23;
  Mythical authority, 58;
  One of five gods in *Ring*, 66;
  Other names,
    9, 15, 34-35, 45, 50;
  Pact with giants, 60-61, 67;
  Relationship in *Ring*,
    134-135;
  Runes, 140;
  Shatters Siegmund's sword,
    90;
  Starts first war, 134;
  Supreme god, 23, 49, 60, 120;
  Swallowed by Fenrir, 138;
  Swears oath on Draupnir,
    105;
  Tears branch from
    World Ash Tree, 20;
  The Changing, 45;
  The Evil Doer, 45;
  The stranger, 14-15, 89;
  Threatened by Donner, 34;
  Thrusts sword into tree,
    89, 96, 97;
  Urge to possess ring, 109;
  Valfader, 76;
  Variations of the name, 121;
  Vidar, his son, 86;
  Wanderer, 50;
  Will cause Loge to break
    into flame, 57;
  Will set the world ablaze, 58;
  Wine his only food, 63, 76;
  Ygg, 15

WOUND BITER,
  A sword, 85

WOUNDING WAND,
  Loge's sword, 87

WRATH,
  Donner's son, 37;
  Siegfried's sword (Gram),
    88-91

WUNSCHMÄDCHEN,
  Valkyries, 76

WUODAN,
  Wotan, 121

WUODEN,
  Wotan, 121

Y

YAWNING GAP,
  Ginnungagap, 17

YDALIR,
  Ull's home, 11

YELLOW SPOTTED, THE,
  Sinfjotli, 90

YEOMAN,
  Karl, 103

YEW (Tree),
  In early Germanic
    culture, 11

YEW DALES,
  Ull's hall, 11

YGG, 15

YGGDRASIL,
  World Ash Tree,
    15-21, 74, 138;
  See also:
    WORLD ASH TREE

YMIR,
  A giant, 7, 9

Studies in The History and Interpretation of Music

1. Hugo Meynell, **The Art of Handel's Operas**

2. Dale A. Jorgenson, **Moritz Hauptmann of Leipzig**

3. Nancy van Deusen, **The Harp and The Soul: Essays in Medieval Music**

4. James L. Taggart, **Franz Joseph Haydn's Keyboard Sonatas: An Untapped Gold Mine**

5. William E. Grim, **The Faust Legend in Music and Literature**

6. Richard R. La Croix (ed.), **Augustine on Music: An Interdisciplinary Collection of Essays**

7. Clifford Taylor, **Musical Idea and the Design Aesthetic in Contemporary Music: A Text for Discerning Appraisal of Musical Thought in Western Culture**

8. Mary Gilbertson, **The Metaphysics of Alliteration in *Pearl***

9. Stephen Barnes, **Muzak—The Hidden Messages in Music: A Social Psychology of Culture**

10. Felix-Eberhard von Cube, **The Book of the Musical Artwork,** David Neumeyer (trans.)

11. Robert G. Luoma, **Music, Mode and Words in Orlando di Lasso's Last Works**

12. John A. Kimmey, **A Critique of Musicology: Clarifying the Scope, Limits and Purposes of Musicology**

13. Kent A. Holliday, **Reproducing Pianos Past and Present**

14. Gloria Shafer, **Origins of the Children's Song Cycle as a Genre with Four Case Studies and an Original Cycle**

15. Bertil von Boer, **Dramatic Cohesion in the Music of Joseph Martin Kraus: From Sacred Music to Symphonic Form**

16. William O. Cord, **The Teutonic Mythology of Richard Wagner's *The Ring of Nibelung*, Volume I: Nine Dramatic Properties**

17. William O. Cord, **The Teutonic Mythology of Richard Wagner's *The Ring of Nibelung*, Volume II: The Family of Gods**

18. William O. Cord, **The Teutonic Mythology of Richard Wagner's *The Ring of Nibelung*, Volume III: The Natural and Supernatural Worlds**

19. Victorien Sardou, *La Tosca*: **Life and Times of a Well Made Thriller**

20. Herbert W. Richardson (ed.), **New Studies in Richard Wagner's** *The Ring of the Nibelungen*

21. Catherine Dower, **Yella Pessl, First Lady of the Harpsichord**

22. Margaret Sheppach, **Dramatic Parallels in the Operas of Michael Tippet**

23. William E. Grim, **Haydn's "Sturm und Drang" Symphonies: Form and Meaning**

24. Anne Trencamp and John G. Suess (eds.), **Studies in the Music of Vienna in the 1920s: A Festschrift in Honor of Marcel Dick**

25. Harold E. Fiske, **Music and Mind: Philosophical Essays on the Cognition and Meaning of Music**

26. Klemens Diez, **Constanze, Formerly Widow of Mozart: Her Unwritten Memoir Based on Historical Documents**, translated and annotated by Joseph Malloy